PRAISE FOR
BUILDING BILLION DOLLAR BRANDS

"When I listened to Rick Cesari's keynote speech at the Prosper Show for Amazon sellers, I couldn't believe how similar his proven process for marketing and developing great products for the direct-to-consumer market was to our process for developing great products for Amazon. I was so impressed by Rick's speech and his long line of enormous commercial successes that I just had to meet him. As it turns out, we both live in Seattle, and since that first meeting, we've developed a wonderful friendship over weekly Seattle coffee. Rick is a wealth of knowledge and a true marketing genius. I continue to learn from him and I share with him my decade and a half of experience selling on the Amazon platform. It still amazes us how well so much of the processes that he developed translate directly into success on Amazon."

Jason Boyce

CEO, Dazadi.com

"If you want to be a successful marketer, buy this book. Barb's extraordinary track record speaks for itself. She instinctively understands what the target consumer wants across different channels and formats. Barb 'gets' the consumer, she knows the buyer, she sells the product. She's a dynamo."

Maria Kalligeros

Kalligeros Communications

"*Barb is one of the most creative, dynamic, and effective marketing genius on the planet. The wisdom and guidance she has to share are priceless.*"

Hank Wuh, MD, MPH

surgeon, inventor, serial entrepreneur
Unicorn Whisperer, Inc.

"*During my time as a CEO of Salton Inc., the company grew from $8 million to $1.4 billion thanks to a team of wonderful individuals who were creative, had the right instincts for finding the right products, and knew how to successfully communicate with consumers. Barbara Westfield and Rick Cesari were two key members of this very successful team. This book, I am sure, will provide the necessary guideposts you need to succeed in the volatile and new retail market we face today.*"

Leon Dreimann

CEO, Greystone Brands, Inc.

"*Branding is tricky—even trickier when building one on a shoe-string budget. However, without a billion-dollar brand strategy, you'll find yourself in a race to the bottom—to your eventual demise.*

With what Rick and Barb outline in this powerful resource, you can immediately enhance the branding of your own business or product, compete against the 'big guys' and do it a lot more profitably!"

Dustin Mathews

chief wealth evangelist, WealthFit.com

"For a number of years Rick has been a guest presenter for my marketing management class at the University of Washington. Rick's presentations on direct response marketing and branding is especially illuminating, as nearly every student in class has, or has used, one of the products Rick has successfully promoted over the years. This practical and approachable content helps the students get what marketing is really all about. Best of all, he has helped me turn students from finance and accounting to marketing!"

Richard Geasey

lecturer, University of Washington Bothell School of Business

"I was looking to interview the top marketers in the world for the InspiredInsider podcast, and when I asked many top entrepreneurs who I should consider, Rick's name kept coming up over and over. I then researched him and found that he has helped sell more than $4 billion worth of product and launched over thirty brands, including Sonicare, Oxiclean, the George Foreman Grill, the Juiceman, the GoPro camera, and many more. His story and journey is quite amazing. If you are just launching a new product or already have an existing product and want to generate more sales, then you should read this book and listen to what Rick says!"

Dr. Jeremy Weisz

founder, InspiredInsider
co-founder, Rise25

"Discipline, data, and determination: Rick and Barb have synthesized thirty years of success building extraordinary household brands into a concise blueprint that every serious brand entrepreneur should be using."

James Thomson, PhD

former head, Amazon Services

co-founder, PROSPER Show, and Brand Authority Summit

partner, Buy Box Experts

author, Amazon Marketplace Dilemma

"I've had the privilege of working with Rick Cesari over the last year on several marketing projects including this book, Building Billion Dollar Brands. What I have found is that Rick is a never-ending source of knowledge that is both fundamental and, at the same time, progressive. He is ever transforming his many years of DRTV and brand experience to new media applications which boosts direct-to-consumer sales. My advice is to devour this book and then stay tuned for more great marketing wisdom from Rick to follow."

Susan Gilbert

CEO, Online Promotion Success, Inc.

"Rick has been an integral marketing partner for my start up, IXIA Sports. He spearheaded our DRTV campaign for our flagship golf training product, TruePendulumMotion, and has propelled us forward to the next level. He is a marketing wizard, and was the missing link to reaching our goals."

Charles Kim

founder and president, IXIA Sports

BUILDING BILLION DOLLAR BRANDS

RICK CESARI & BARB WESTFIELD

BUILDING
BILLION DOLLAR
BRANDS

SPECTACULAR SUCCESSES & CAUTIONARY TALES:
THE LURE OF BRAND RESPONSE FROM BOTH SIDES
OF THE MARKETING FENCE

Published by Advantage, Charleston, South Carolina.
Member of Advantage Media Group.

ADVANTAGE is a registered trademark, and the Advantage colophon is a trademark of Advantage Media Group, Inc.

Printed in the United States of America.

10 9 8 7 6 5 4 3 2 1

ISBN: 978-1-59932-702-0
LCCN: 2018958851

Cover design by Melanie Cloth.
Layout design by Megan Elger.

This publication is designed to provide accurate and authoritative information in regard to the subject matter covered. It is sold with the understanding that the publisher is not engaged in rendering legal, accounting, or other professional services. If legal advice or other expert assistance is required, the services of a competent professional person should be sought.

Advantage Media Group is proud to be a part of the Tree Neutral® program. Tree Neutral offsets the number of trees consumed in the production and printing of this book by taking proactive steps such as planting trees in direct proportion to the number of trees used to print books. To learn more about Tree Neutral, please visit **www.treeneutral.com**.

Advantage Media Group is a publisher of business, self-improvement, and professional development books and online learning. We help entrepreneurs, business leaders, and professionals share their Stories, Passion, and Knowledge to help others Learn & Grow. Do you have a manuscript or book idea that you would like us to consider for publishing? Please visit **advantagefamily.com** or call **1.866.775.1696**.

RICK CESARI

To Martha, my loving wife who keeps me focused
on what's important in life.

BARB WESTFIELD

To my father, Charles Augustus Westfield, Sr., who taught me early on
that it's always better to sell a gross rather than a dozen.

ACKNOWLEDGMENTS

RICK:

❝ One of my favorite mantras is, "Success has many fathers, but failure is an orphan." This could not be truer when talking about some of the iconic brands that we have helped build. There were always great people, product owners, and management teams involved with every big success along the way. Here are just a few of the many people we worked with that we would like to acknowledge, listed in chronological order based on the time frame we worked on each brand:

Steve Cesari and Robert Lamson, my partners in Trillium Health products (the Juiceman and Breadman Brands); Jay Kordich, the original Juiceman; and Dan Riley for introducing us and editing many of our successful shows. David Sabin and Leon Dreimann, the respective chairman and CEO of Salton Housewares, and the makers of the George Foreman Grill and the Rejuvenique facial toning mask. David Guiliani, David Engel, Eric Meyer, Mike Stull, and Bill McClain, founders and management team of Optiva corp., the makers of Sonicare. Jane Schloth, president of Cesari Response Television, my right-hand person for over twenty years and the founder/CEO of Direct Branding. Max and Elaine Appel, Joel and David Appel, the founders of Orange Glo International, the makers of OxiClean, Orange Glo, Orange Clean, and Kaboom. Spokesperson Billy Mays. Jim Sorensen, founder of Momentus Golf. Tim Wall and Steve Wahl, the CEO and the marketing director of Rug Doctor. Nick Woodman, the founder of GoPro. **"**

BARB:

" To the mentors I've learned from in my career: at Bullocks department stores, Michael Steinberg, Mark Grand, and Terry Lundgren. During my many years at Salton, Leon Dreimann, Bert Doornmalen, David Sabin, and my colleagues there. To this day, we're a tight knit crew. Thanks for the opportunities. I've relished working with visionaries at HoMedics, Eades Appliance Technology—specifically the Drs. Eades. I recently had the pleasure of working with a remarkable young executive, Megan Nehls, at Johnsonville Sausage. The caliber of her work and her professional demeanor made me better at my job. Lastly to Wolfgang Puck, with whom I stood side by side at the stoves at Spago, Beverly Hills, when he remarked to me, "Always put the mushrooms in last, and don't f**k it up with too many flavors." **"**

TABLE OF CONTENTS

FOREWORD

I first met Barbara in the early eighties when she was on the buying side of small kitchen appliances at Federated Department Stores and I was on the development, procurement, and supply side of the SDA industry in the US.

Barb taught me the fundamentals of what consumers were looking for in brand name products, and she continued to be my source of inspiration and know-how during the ensuing years.

Times were different then, and product cycles took a while to be developed and come to market, but since then the world has changed, and one of the main drivers for consumers remains intact: the consumers' trust in brands. But even that is now also undergoing changes due to the emerging "sharing economy" and the new ways brands have to adapt to rapid shifts in a customer base with technology-forward millennials entering their earning years and maturing Gen Xers becoming more technology-savvy and less loyal to the habits and brands of their forebears.

This means that once more brands have to reinvent themselves to stay relevant, and they must become proactive in engaging with today's end users in such a way that they can capitalize on their rich history and at the same time create such a social awareness that they become the foremost and first to go to source for the "new consumer of today."

Barb and Rick's book illustrates the multiple changes brands went through in the preceding thirty-five years, and how brands coped with changing consumer demands and managed the consumer's expectations. This will continue, even though the very nature of the brands is that they adopt slower to changing market conditions due to their hierarchical structures, but in the end they will always catch up because of their rich heritage. Those brands will then prevail if they embrace the new sharing economy.

The books illustrates the changes of the past and how the brands managed. I am looking forward to the sequel ten years from now.

Bert Doornmalen

INTRODUCTION

BY RICK CESARI

"A business is simply an idea to make other people's lives better."

—Richard Branson

I have always had a passion for healthy eating. I think that sprung from the fact that my father passed away from a heart attack when he was only forty-five years old, mostly from lifestyle issues that were preventable. I was just twelve years old at the time, and as one of eight brothers and sisters I was always focused on what I could do to get ahead. In 1989, me and my brother Steve started a company called JM Marketing. The JM stood for "Juiceman," my idea of a great name at the time. I did not know a thing about branding, but we were going to teach people about the benefits of drinking fresh fruit and vegetable juices as a way to improve health. One of my passions then and now is customer service; every customer would be treated the way I would want to be treated if I was considering buying a product or had issues with a product I already bought. I call this simple concept, "The Golden Rule of Branding," which we will talk more about it later in the book.

The company became highly successful in a very short period of time, growing to over $75 million in sales in only four years. Then, in 1993, three really great things happened: (1) we sold the business to a company in Chicago, called Salton Housewares, (2) I met Barb Westfield, the CMO of Salton at that time, and (3) I learned that a powerful brand equals freedom.

Barb and I have now worked together on and off for almost twenty-five years, helping to build many household brands from scratch—products you use in your home every day, like the George Foreman Grill, (our first billion-dollar brand), Sonicare, (our second billion-dollar brand), OxiClean (our third billion-dollar brand), Clarisonic, Rug Doctor, GoPro (our fourth billion-dollar brand), and many more. This book is about the valuable lessons we learned in building these brands and many others. We will be sharing these experiences with you so that you can learn from both our successes and our mistakes. This isn't theory to be taught in a classroom; these are real-life strategies that we have used successfully over the last twenty-five years that are constantly being updated and evolved based on what is working in today's marketplace.

You'll be introduced to what we call our Five Keys to Building a Great Brand. Marketing techniques, retailers, and distribution channels have changed dramatically since we started twenty-five-plus years ago, and they will continue to change, but we have found that these five keys remain constant. They create a simple foundation that, when applied, work in every instance. We both still use these key foundational principals with every product we launch and every client we work with. In this book we will expand on these simple brand-building keys and show you how you can put them to use immediately in your business or new product launch.

THE FIVE KEYS TO BUILDING A GREAT BRAND

1. USP—Identify your "unique selling proposition."

2. Positioning—Create a name and market position for your product or business.

3. Deliver Value—Under-promise, over-deliver.

4. Listen to Your Customers—Develop world-class customer service and powerful testimonials that will sell for you 24/7.

5. Direct Branding—The best way to brand for most small businesses and startups.

Many people have never heard the term "direct branding," but it is the best description of the type of marketing we have been using for the last twenty-five years. We were the pioneers in this area of advertising in building both the Juiceman and Breadman brands, which combines traditional brand-building techniques with highly measurable direct response advertising to create a powerful hybrid model that sells product while you are building the brand. Every advertising dollar spent is accountable and this lets you generate revenue from day one. Direct branding is the secret weapon that evens the playing field with large companies that have massive advertising budgets. It is how new startups like Sonicare beat Braun, and how OxiClean beat Clorox—as well as Procter and Gamble—at their own game. Direct branding is even easier today with all of the additional online marketing platforms at your disposal, as long as you understand the concept that direct-to-consumer selling is brand building. Anytime you do marketing it is always with a direct response mindset and with the goal of bringing in two dollars in revenue for every one dollar spent on advertising, regardless of the marketing channel being used.

We are teaching you the underlying strategies for direct brand building, not the specific tactics. Marketing is constantly changing, and while we primarily used direct response TV advertising and a good public relations strategy to build the Juiceman, Sonicare, and OxiClean brands, more recently we have used digitally-based content marketing, such as online video, YouTube, and social platforms to help build the SousVide Supreme and GoPro brands. Yet, the Five Keys to Building a Great Brand remain the same and are still implemented as the foundational element for each brand.

—RICK CESARI

CHAPTER ONE

What Is a Brand and Why Do You Need One?

"A branding program should be designed to differentiate your cow from all the other cattle on the range, even if all the other cattle on the range look pretty much alike."

—Al Ries, author, *New Positioning: The Battle for Your Mind Escalates*

We'll be talking a lot more about brands and brand building in this book—but first, what is a brand, really? A brand is simply the identity by which a customer comes to recognize a product, service, or function. Sometimes a very successful brand supersedes its specific product and becomes synonymous with the category itself, like Kleenex, Jell-O, or Band-Aids.

But what differentiates a powerful, memorable, and successful brand from one that simply fails to catch fire, or to get the attention of the consumer? Here's a hint: it's not necessarily the fault of the product in question. Rather, it's in how it's packaged and presented—and that's the power of branding.

BARB:

" A great illustration of this philosophy comes from my experience with an electric appliance, one that initially came to market with the name the Fajita Express. Its Chinese manufacturers first brought it to my office when I was a vice president of marketing at Salton. A tabletop grill, the Fajita Express was taxicab yellow with a graphic of a longhorn steer on top. The guys showed me a camcorder video that showed the appliance cooking meat; the fat from the protein was rendered into drippings, which ran into an attached sloped pan. A spatula with grooves allowed the user to easily fill taco shells with the cooked meat. Since Salton was always actively sourcing new products, I brought the Fajita Express to my boss, Leon Dreimann, the CEO of Salton. While the product didn't elicit much enthusiasm with my colleagues, we decided to take the product to a trade show and demo it to see how retailers responded.

It was a flop. No retailers wanted it. Fajitas simply weren't going to move the needle, so back it went to the corporate HQ in Chicago, where I boxed up all the samples and documents and put them into storage. A few months later, Leon came into my office and asked, "Barbs, remember that grill from the show? Pack it all up, everything, and send it off to this guy."

"This guy," was Mike Shrednick, whom I knew from my days as a buyer at Bullock's. Mike was renowned in the Los Angeles retail community for his groundbreaking store, the Shrednick Collection, and for his influence as a pioneer selling goods from mainland China.

Glad to get the Fajita Express out of my sample storage room, I packed it up and sent the grill and all of the documents off to Mike in Los Angeles. Several months later in January of 1995 I was called into a top-level meeting with Leon and key members of our sales team. From behind his desk, Leon asked, "Remember that grill? It's coming back, and it's going to be tied to a celebrity, so we have to be ready. I can't tell you who it is, but if it happens, it's going to be big."

About three weeks later we were called back to Leon's office to talk about the grill again. This time, we were told that the branding for the grill was going to feature the boxer George Foreman; he simply loved hamburgers, so George had asked his representatives to find him a product that made them. He liked his burgers a little too much, actually. His weight had gone up, and now he'd become health conscious. The former Fajita Express grilled hamburgers really well, plus the fat-rendering qualities of the sample product appealed to him, so it was rebranded as a tool that a lovable, aspirational athlete could use to cook the foods he loved guilt-free.

This case study is an example of extreme rapid cycle branding and identity development: January of 1995 we were given that initial heads up. February of 1995 we were told it was George and that we had about five weeks to get ready for a huge launch at the Gourmet Products Show in Las Vegas. When the time came, all systems were go, except George Foreman was slated to fight a boxer in Germany named Axel Schulz on April 22, so he was in training and not to be disturbed. His big fight and this major tradeshow were two weeks apart, which meant we were facing a pressure-driven ticking clock. To make matters more complicated, we no longer had any samples, as they were with Foreman's various attorneys and George. But we made it happen with a great deal of ingenuity on the fly. Trade magazine and PR closing dates were in March, and new samples had to be made by the factory. That's how the Fajita Express was transformed and rebranded into the Lean, Mean, Fat-Reducing Grilling Machine.

Under those insane deadlines and a year after I had been introduced to the original Fajita Express, Salton went back to the Gourmet Products tradeshow in Las Vegas with the rebranded grill. George flew in for appearances and we shot all the content assets right there in the Las Vegas Convention Center, one week after his winning fight against Axel Schulz.

George strode through the Las Vegas Convention Center like Moses parting the Red Sea—this tall, powerful, mountain of a man passed confidently through the adoring crowd who followed him eagerly as he approached the booth where his eponymous Foreman Grill was on display. 🙾

RICK:

🙾 Barb and I worked together to produce the very first infomercial for the George Foreman Grill and had it on the air in the fall of 1995. It made history with well over one hundred million units sold, which is perhaps the largest selling TV product of all time.

What had changed? Not the product itself in any significant way; we made it white instead of yellow and created the Lean, Mean, Fat-Reducing Grilling Machine logo. We put George's signature on there so it had an autograph, and came up with the unique selling proposition (USP) line, "Knock out the fat!" That trademark became the story, and that story caught fire. Suddenly, George's Lean, Mean, Fat-Reducing Grilling Machine was showing up everywhere, even on *Sex & the City*. Oprah raved about how her family loved cooking bacon with it, and word of mouth just got bigger and bigger. The *New York Times*'s Suzanne Hamlin wrote a story about its convenience for folks trying to keep their New Year's diet resolutions.[1] Food writers for prominent publications began covering the Grill as an essential kitchen appliance, elevating the product in terms of its validity in the foodie world. We ran a Super Bowl spot during halftime. This handy product quickly became about more than burgers—you could grill an amazing salmon fillet in three and a half minutes. The grill took on a personality of its own: a healthy, fast, fun way to cook all kinds of popular foods. **"**

BARB:

" Leon's moniker of the Lean, Mean, Fat-Reducing Grilling Machine became an iconic slogan. Once I met George in the Seattle airport in the late '90s, when a high school baseball team came walking by and spotted him. The kids yelled out in admiration, "Hey, it's the Lean, Mean, Fat-Reducing Grilling Machine!" **"**

RICK:

" For many of our early brand building and business growth successes we used thirty-minute direct response infomercials. Why? Two reasons: First was the length; if you were trying to sell someone something, would you rather have thirty minutes to explain the product, or thirty seconds? Common sense, isn't it? Second, we were able to reach large audiences in a very cost-effective way. Direct response advertising did not appeal to all consumers but we were looking for the ones it did appeal to, and this was an easy and cheap way to reach them. If people are interested in what you are saying,

---

1   Suzanne Hamlin, "Test Kitchen; A Grill That Keeps the Moistness, Drains the Fat" *New York Times*, December 31, 1997, https://www.nytimes.com/1997/12/31/dining/test-kitchen-a-grill-that-keeps-the-moistness-drains-the-fat.html.

they will stop and listen. Our goal is to build a database of happy customers that we can remarket to in the future. Remember, some of these campaigns were done before there was ecommerce or Amazon.

So, what does a campaign like this look like in today's marketing stack? We'd use a thirty-second TV spot or Facebook ads to drive people to a website where they have the time and space to absorb the messaging and buy. The common denominator between these two tactics? A direct response ad is being used to convert your customer to take action and push them into the sales funnel.

Now is a good time to dispel a myth: advertising is a method of getting people to purchase things they don't want or need.

Here's the truth—humans want and need products and services. It's a basic primal drive, this instinctive urge to engage in tool making and hunting/gathering. From our ancient ancestors to our digital lives today, these deep instincts ensure we're always on the lookout for something external that will help us live better, happier lives. Filtering, assessing, and acquisition are ineradicable human traits. Being consumers in the prehistoric sense is what preserved us from being consumed in the literal sense. Even in the age of decluttering and minimalism, we're still feathering our nests.

There is a grain of truth to this myth—clearly not *everyone* needs *every* product. But if you have a quality product, you owe it to your prospective customers to do everything ethically possible to make sure they have the opportunity to benefit. Not doing so is the real disservice you should avoid. You can't create positive transformations if you never offer consumers that chance.

The initial infomercial we made for the George Foreman Grill told the story very clearly—the story that the original developers of the device simply hadn't seen as important. In our infomercial, we showed hamburgers cooking in a frying pan in a bath of their own grease. And we showed what that fat looked like when it cooled, congealed, and solidified—certainly not appetizing. That visual asked the question, "Would you rather cook your burger like this or would you rather remove some of the fat and the grease?" The unique selling proposition—the USP, and brand building key number one—was that you could "knock out the fat" by cooking foods quickly and easily while removing the excess unhealthy fat and grease at the same time. That's what made this grill different from anything else out there at the time. The new product name said it all—the George Foreman Lean, Mean, Fat-Reducing Grilling Machine—and the hero shot was a close-up of the front of the grill while hamburgers were cooking and the excess grease and fat dripped away from the food. Who wouldn't want that? Between the health benefits, the cooking convenience, and the appeal of George's personality, this former ugly duckling of a product was transformed into one of the most iconic small appliances of all time—thanks to great branding and product re-positioning. 🙶

How You Can Use a Brand to Differentiate Yourself in a Crowded Marketplace

Clearly things have changed since the rebranding of the Fajita Express. Twenty-one years ago, we had a longer lead time in which to make an impression. Today, with the impact of Omnichannel and social media marketing, how/where/why consumers will find your product is radically different; now product information is literally at their—

and your—fingertips. When we started with the George Foreman Grill, it was the Internet version of horse and buggy days. We once had to wait up to six months to gather consumer data from warranty card registrations to discover who was buying the product and what their motivation was for buying. What was the buyers' demographic profile and psychographic profile? Why were they buying? Today, that information is available within seconds.

BARB:

66 Who is your customer, and where do they live? When, where, and why do they shop? Your ability to understand the *who* and *why* of your customer base is critical. In a start-up or seedling environment, please use every single available data intelligence tool that is available. The baseline is Google Analytics (GA), SEO/PPC competitive bidding, and visibility on any and all social media platforms. Social media, content creation, and GA should not be a sideline position in your marketing department or a summer intern's job. And, as simple as a warranty registration, address book, or loyalty program may seem, you can garner more data about your consumer (with their permission, of course) and use that to begin building your fan base for outreach and community. If you choose not to employ this critical path business tactic you will be left in your competitors' dust. 99

RICK:

66 Ten years ago, it took so long to create a product that you also had time to build a brand. But now, for example with Amazon, there are people who will look for the bestselling product in a certain

category. Consider a product like a blender. A seller sees that everyone is buying blenders. So, they go to Alibaba or some other source in China and find a lower-priced manufacturer for blenders. The next thing you know, there are six or seven people selling blenders on Amazon. Everybody is fighting over the "buy box"; it's called a "race to the bottom" because you are competing on price alone, not any kind of product differentiation or branding. Whoever can bring the product in for the least cost and sell it at the lowest price on Amazon wins. There is nothing unique about the product or packaging, there is no branding, and it's a margin killer. Worst of all, you are unable to create a long-term relationship with the people who are buying your products—your customers.

The big question of branding in such a market environment is: How do you set your product apart from everybody else's so that when people think of that product or category they'll buy your product and even pay more for it? In our consulting business, we work with a lot of Amazon sellers, helping them to create their brand identity outside of Amazon and to build a powerful database of happy customers willing to purchase their next product offering. This requires a multi-step marketing approach under the umbrella of direct response marketing, as illustrated here:

360 SALES ACCELERATOR

If you really want to engage your consumer—and you're at a prestige level where you're talking about a price point transaction over $50, $60, $100, or higher—it's an entirely different approach. This branding requires **brand trust**. The higher the retail price, the higher the quotient of brand trust has to be. A strong relationship with your customer is vital and something that is hard to create directly through Amazon alone; we'll discuss this in more detail later on.

Introducing the Juiceman

A relevant example is how we approached changing the market viewpoint around fresh fruit and vegetable juicers with Juiceman. We introduced the Juiceman juice extractor in 1989. Up until then, German companies such as Braun and Krups dominated the consumer marketplace for juicers, and the demand in the USA and Canada for juicers and drinking fresh juice was minimal at that point. The German companies were marketing juicers as a household appliance, and the product pitch was about the features of the machines themselves: powerful motors, stainless steel blades, and dishwasher safe plastics, all crafted with German engineering.

With the Juiceman juicer, we didn't talk about the features. Instead, we educated people about the benefits you would gain from drinking fresh juice, such as how drinking freshly extracted juices could help them, for instance, live longer, have more energy, build immune strength, and lower cholesterol. Focusing on the health benefits

Remember the old saying: "Features tell and benefits sell!"

of the juice and not the features of the machine is what attracted people to the Juiceman product and created a powerful brand. We were able to differentiate our juicer from the other juicers in the marketplace just by focusing on the benefits of the fresh juice. Remember the old saying: "Features tell and benefits sell!" This simple concept created the whole fresh juice movement you see in the marketplace today and also created exponential sales growth for the parent company, Trillium Health Products.

Good branding and marketing can have a powerful positive impact on society. I like to think that we helped many millions of people to question and ultimately change their food choices for the better, to start taking the steps toward living a healthier lifestyle, and to reap all the resulting health benefits.

The other secret we used to build a powerful brand was to create a dynamic spokesperson for the whole juicing movement. Jay Kordich, the father of modern juicing, sold juicers door to door and at small health food stores all across the country for over twenty years. He would go to a city, sell a few machines, and then move on to the next market. Because of this he was the perfect spokesperson for the Juiceman brand. We were able to magnify through our innovative marketing the same message he was delivering to small groups, amplifying it to a larger national audience. Enlisting a dynamic spokesperson who can help you brand your product is a powerful strategy, which we will discuss in more detail in later chapters. We also used this marketing technique with George Foreman and with Billy Mays and OxiClean. There's also more detail about how we built the Juiceman business in my first book, *Buy Now: Creative Marketing that Gets Customers to Respond to You and Your Product*.

Would You Pay $150 for a Toothbrush?

Another branding challenge at the prestige level was the introduction of the Sonicare toothbrush. The manufacturers were having a tough time getting it distributed at retail because it was $150, and in 1995 there weren't any other electric toothbrushes selling at that price point. The average price point for a manual toothbrush was less than $3. The fact that it had new technology and a powerful USP— "Cleans beyond the bristles"—didn't matter to consumers, because they did not understand the benefits that the technology provided. They saw the price tag and walked away.

We recognized that if we could we get consumers to see the benefits, the price would no longer be a factor. What was required was an educational component; so, we educated people about the health dangers of gum disease and how the Sonicare technology, which got into the nooks and crannies of their teeth, could help to prevent or even reverse periodontitis (gum disease). We guaranteed, "Better dental check-ups or your money back!" Once the consumer understood that using the new Sonicare technology would improve the health of their teeth and gums and result in better dental check-ups, they happily paid the premium price for it.

With Sonicare and most of the other products we work with, it's critical to get the product into the hands of what we call "key opinion leaders," or influencers. With Sonicare, those influencers were the top dentists and periodontists in the country; with the George Foreman Grill and SousVide Supreme, those influencers were the top chefs and food writers using the product. These influencers have the ability to reach a large, dedicated following and create endorsed awareness for your product. People like to follow what the leaders in a category are doing.

What's Your Unique Selling Proposition?

Your unique selling proposition—brand building key number one—should illustrate the kind of authentic backstory your product needs to have in order to stand out in the crowded marketplace. Find a "niche" or "category" that distinguishes you from the competition. Sally Hogshead, the author of a great book called *Fascinate,* coined the phrase, "Different is better than 'better!'" Sonicare wasn't just a better toothbrush; it was better because it was so different from what was out there at the time.

This is what's often referred to as the "blue ocean strategy," after the excellent book of the same name by authors W. Chan Kim and Renee Mauborgne. Find the wide-open area with no competition in view—the blue ocean—and claim it as your space. If you can position your product in that space so that you're not competing with any other products, you have the whole market to yourself. The George Foreman Grill did this by being the only grill product of its kind that made the claim about reducing fat in food; Sonicare did it by being the only electric toothbrush that could clean beyond the bristles with clinical data supporting its claims that using it reduced gum disease. 🙿

Your unique selling proposition—brand building key number one—should illustrate the kind of authentic backstory your product needs to have in order to stand out in the crowded marketplace. Find a "niche" or "category" that distinguishes you from the competition.

What Happens When All the Stars Align, and Then the Lights Go Out?

Just being unique and ahead of your time isn't enough when luck doesn't line up on your side, however. A case in point was the skincare device called Rejuvenique, a great product that was way ahead of its time—and unfortunately the timing was lousy.

BARB:

❝ Rejuvenique was a genuinely unique product, albeit one that suffered to some extent because of what we call "founder's syndrome."

Founders and inventors nearly always believe strongly in their own products—so much so that often they're incapable of seeing that their baby has limitations or other challenges that are going to make it a difficult sale to consumers.

What do I mean by this? Well, let's take an inventory of the merchandising potential of a product:

- Is the technology new or unique to the consumer side of business, e.g. is it coming from industrial, commercial, or medical roots?

- Is there an existing merchandising category that the product fits into at retail? Or is the type of technology so unique that the buyer has to really be behind your product/ brand, story, and advertising campaign to give you shelf and e-com space?

- What is the price point at retail?

- Has the inventor third-party tested the product, and are the claims substantiated or can they be?

- Has it passed or can it pass any and all compliance and safety requirements which retailers demand?

- Does the product have any inherent traits that could trigger cultural issues? Sound crazy? It can happen.

This last point was certainly the case with this high-end beauty product, a skin-rejuvenating electric impulse facial mask called Rejuvenique. It looked a lot like a hockey mask; so much so that the *Friday the 13th* jokes started to pop up everywhere. Having a beauty product that garnered loads of jokes and ridicule from comedians created a major hurdle.

While the inventors had conducted qualitative testing in which women tried the product and liked the result, we prepared to go to market and were obliged to do much more in-depth testing. We went through efficacy testing for the reduction of wrinkles, improved firmness and skin tone, as well as safety testing at leading universities. Salton spent close to $1 million to produce and ship a prestige level beauty product with a full package of FDA compliance, legal, and marketing support, including an infomercial to tell the story of how electrical toning of the facial muscles could reduce wrinkles and help improve firmness in the face.

We signed the television star Linda Evans of *Dynasty* to host our infomercial. Rick's company did the media test, and to this day the results we saw from those initial tests were among the highest we'd ever seen, surpassing even the George Foreman Grill. Everything was aligning to turn this product into a huge success. At last, we overcame all the thresholds for the coveted FDA review and got clearance.

Forty-eight hours later, Botox was cleared.

Rejuvenique works and our clinical trials proved this—but it takes time to work. Botox takes a couple of injections and less than twenty-four hours later facial lines are gone. In our "instant results" culture, Botox was a no-brainer choice for the consumer. That was the first blow, followed by the second previously mentioned: the release of the *Friday the 13th* movie, featuring a serial killer who wore—you guessed it—a white hockey mask that made him look a lot like someone using our wonderful product.

Here we had a great product, one that really worked, but it was in the wrong place at the wrong time. Today, beauty and cosmetics retailers sell all kinds of high-end beauty devices to improve skin tone and clarity, including dozens of high tech masks for facial rejuvenation, because women realized that Botox wasn't the answer to every challenge. As of this writing, a major skin care company is marketing a plastic facial mask across multiple media platforms and it's on the shelf at major chain drug stores. Sometimes being ahead of your time isn't the best place to be—particularly if you're way too early. And in those circumstances, no matter how great a job you're doing with your branding, it's just not going to work. **99**

YOUR BRANDING Q AND A: WHAT ARE THE BRAND ATTRIBUTES, ETHICS, AND POSITION?

These three items taken together create what is called the UX—the user experience. When you're looking at your product and trying to define what your brand is, here are some questions that you need to consider:

1. **What are your brand's ethics?**

When we're talking about ethics in today's marketplace, what exactly does that mean? The first requirement is that the product is ethically produced—no child labor, no questionably sourced ingredients. Does it do good in the world, or does it harm? Take Ben and Jerry's ice cream with its ethically sourced ingredients, or Tom's shoes, a brand that gives a pair of shoes to someone in a developing nation for every pair sold. Nike ReGrind recycles old plastic into new shoe soles. Where and how you produce your product matters to its story and to your storytelling. Consider the social mores in today's marketplace that might make a consumer think twice about your product. Is it safety? Is it recycling?

Is it supporting a charitable cause on some level? Is it helping another person, like Tom's shoes? Is it sustainably raised, like farmed fish, or free of hormones, like organic chicken? Part of creating a dynamic brand is the image and perception your company has on a personal level. It's what you stand for and it allows you to tell your clients a story that creates an emotional attachment.

2.   **What's your brand's position?**

Is it mass market? Is it mid-range? Is it prestige? Knowing where your product fits and who your consumer is likely to be has everything to do with how you'll brand it.

3.   **What are your product's attributes?**

By attributes, we mean your product specifications—the technology of it and how it pushes your buttons, what it makes you feel like. Do you feel better having a coffee from a Keurig or a Nespresso? Do you feel better in flip-flops from Old Navy or wearing Havaianas?

Basic Steps for Smart Branding Are:

Think Big from the Start.

If you're building a brand from the ground up, assume it's going to be big. Why? Because as with anything else in life, you'll achieve your outcomes based on the picture that you paint. So, if you only see your product as being sold in a corner store and you can't envision it being sold by a major retailer, then you've drawn a very small circle for yourself. If you want to run a multi-million-dollar business, you have to look at it differently, starting with good fundamentals.

Maybe your plan for your product is to sell it exclusively online, which is fine. But it's going from the pushcart to a much broader audience. A good example was my original name for the Juicer business: calling the company JM Marketing was very limiting. So, after we reached $10 million in sales, we changed the name to Trillium Health Products as an umbrella company and were able to add more healthy eating brands like the Breadman.

Do the Research; Listen to the Customer.

Get your product together with your consumer—either your current customer if your product is already on the market, or your potential customer if you're in the pre-launch stage. Start with what we call anthropological (hands-on) studies; give your product to people who are willing to be perfectly honest with you and have them use your product and report back. Listen to them, get your ego out of the way, and act on what you're told (not just what you hear). If your product is already out in the marketplace and you have customers or clients using your product, their feedback is an invaluable tool. The very first step in the process from a market standpoint should be interviewing twenty to thirty people that have been using the product and asking them a series of twenty to thirty questions. Based on the answers you receive, you come out knowing exactly what their motivations were for buying the product, but also the things they didn't like about the product. We have found that this is the best way to do market research without spending a fortune. You get honest feedback from people that paid money for your product, versus giving it away to product reviewers or focus group panelists that have no skin in the game. When we are building the marketing program that defines a brand, unfiltered feedback helps us frame our pitch. These days you don't have to go any further than your Amazon product reviews, at least initially. This approach requires you to be willing to listen and act on what you're told, even if it's not what you wanted or expected to hear. Don't be undone by founder's syndrome.

Start with the End in Mind.

We often meet founders or inventors who want to bring a product to the market, but at the end of the day there are many other contributing factors to success beyond branding and marketing. Success also requires having a solid supply chain and working capital. If your endgame is to have a product that's the most amazing new product in the world, and you want to sell a million pieces, then the preparation is getting the right factories, getting the right supply chain, etc. so that you've got the solid, well-crafted framework ready to support your marketing and sales plan. The most successful businesses don't reach that status by accident. They choose their destination in advance and work toward it in everything they do. Businesses without a clear destination jump reactively from one opportunity to another without any consistent strategy and usually without moving the business forward. A clear business destination sets the foundational direction for all activity in a company. It outlines the business focus and key strategies to achieve success.

Nail Down Your Product's Name and Packaging.

This is such an important part of the process; however, it is often neglected—to the detriment of the product. We worked recently with a New York physician and company founder who'd come up with a terrific product but it didn't have the right packaging. The problem was that the product itself was very, very tiny—the size of a pinky finger. But it was priced as a prestige product, retailing at $100, so now they had to go backward and create a packaging hierarchy so that their item could actually ship to retail and be merchandised effectively. Your packaging is the platform on which the customer first sees your product physically in their hands. What differentiates it? It might be the substrate. It could be the finish. It could be the kind of ink. Is it soft touch? Is it matte? Is it a window box? All of these choices matter a lot, particularly when the product itself is so small. The packaging has to sell it. The goal is to make people fall in love with your product from just the packaging alone. You are selling the experience, as Apple does with all their products. The unboxing experience needs to be remarkable.

Don't Forget the Trademark, the Registration, and the IP.

You've created a wonderful product, you're working on your marketing, and you've picked out a name for your product only to discover that another company is already using it. What do you do? If you've already spent money on a marketing campaign based on that name, you could be out of pocket. That's why it's critical to first visit the website for the United States Patent and Trademark Office and do a trademark search to make sure that your mark is unused. This is more important than ever, because predatory sellers will swoop down and grab a name or trademark that's been allowed to lapse. Recently a Chinese company did exactly that to a brand of French sweets, Calissons, a brand that has existed for over two hundred years in France, originating in Aix en Provence. Now they're producing a look-alike confection under the same famous name, and there's not much the original producers can do about it except to dig deep into their legal budget.[2]

Be Wary of URL Squatters.

"URL squatters" buy up multiple versions of your brand name's URL and holds them hostage, such as variations on your webpage name with .org, .com, .net, or .biz following, depending on which you do not own already. Acquiring those ahead of time is cheap insurance to secure your name.

Don't Be Too Clever When Coming Up with a Name.

Back in the '60s and '70s when a product was named or branded, it was usually quite literal. Today, there's a lot of poetic license taken in grammar and spelling of brand names. They may seem witty and savvy, but what does the name mean across the board culturally? It could have a completely different meaning in another subset demographic group that might find it offensive. We were working on a product recently and the naming agency came up with a whole slew of names that were variations on a theme, using imaginative spellings—yet every single one of them had an issue. In today's omnichannel world where Facebook, Instagram, Google, and Twitter, are the instant news outlets, it doesn't matter that you're located in the United States, because the border is open when you visit the Internet. The company's founder of the product we were working with discovered that the brand name he loved was already attached to a very large company in another country. Even though it's not registered in

---

2   Surbhi Kapila, "French Confectioners Turn Bitter Over the Sweet of Calisson Chinese Firm Hogging the Limelight over French Sweet," Media India Group, November 18, 2016, https://mediaindia.eu/freestyle/ french-confectioners-turn-bitter-over-the-sweet-of-calisson/.

this country, using the name would be rife with all kinds of legal and online search hurdles. Just the difficulties attached to doing SEO and pay-per-click for the name they wanted were financially insurmountable. Products of ours such as the Juiceman, Breadman, Sonicare, Clarisonic, the George Foreman Grill, Oxiclean, Rug Doctor, GoPro, Natural Stacks, Momentus Golf, Squish, Brethe, and DermaFlash all have names that became dominant and transitioned into brands. They are all simple and descriptive names that kicked their brands into high gear. You have to consider the look, feel, and personality of the *brand*, not your own personality—that's founder's syndrome. Not everybody's going to like you, so settle for making them like the product.

> *You have to consider the look, feel, and personality of the brand, not your own personality—that's founder's syndrome. Not everybody's going to like you, so settle for making them like the product.*

Summary

Brand building does not have to be complicated. Just follow the simple tips outlined in this chapter, use them from the very beginning, and be consistent with your use, and you will be well on the way to creating a great brand.

CHAPTER TWO

Direct Branding: Don't Brand to Create Sales, Sell to Create the Brand

"The aim of marketing is to know and understand the customer so well the product or service fits them and sells itself."

—Peter Drucker, author, thought leader

The reason we've put this chapter early in our book despite direct branding being brand building key number five is because marketing and sales are crucial to building your brand. You can't create your brand in a vacuum without consumer feedback and expect it to be a success. We know it is better to use our experience and gut instinct to shape the brand identity and then release it to the consumer as a test and let them tell us what they like and don't like. The only way to test is to activate the sales runway. We always use some form of direct response advertising simply because it works on multiple levels.

In order to understand the evolution of direct brand advertising, let's go back to the dark ages of television—literally. Those of you old enough to remember those days will recall that every night at around eleven o'clock the color bars, test pattern, or the picture of the flag that came up to signal the end of the broadcast day. Then, the Federal Trade Commission and the FCC made a groundbreaking ruling: the "dark time" could now be used for programming or commercials. This opened up seven to eight hours of new commercial time for TV stations, so they started selling these blocks of time they had no programming to fill.

Further deregulation occurred during the Reagan years, when the rules—which had limited advertising to eight minutes per broadcast hour—were overturned. This made it possible for stations to run the long form ads we call infomercials, which previously had been shorter, low-budget ads mainly for household products like vegetable choppers. Now, large inventories of ad space were suddenly available for bargain basement prices.

The worlds of brand advertising and direct response advertising were wholly separate at this point. Direct response advertising was nicknamed "yell and sell," since on-air talent on those early spots imitated the style of old-fashioned carny barkers. In fact, many of those personalities came directly from the country fair circuits. They were chasing fast sales, not trying to build brands.

What is Direct Response Advertising, and How is it Different from Brand Advertising?

In brand advertising, the primary purpose is to create awareness; in direct response advertising, the aims are both to sell and to create new customers right away. Here is an info-graphic that does a great job of pointing out the difference between branding and direct response advertising:

DIRECT RESPONSE VERSUS BRANDING
WHICH IS YOUR CAMPAIGN STRATEGY?

Objectives dictate what kind of digital campaign a brand should launch. There are two main types of digital campaigns:

1. BRANDING   2. DIRECT RESPONSE

A branding campaign works if you're looking to build brand recognition in the marketplace, increase website traffic, and engage your target audience in a natural online environment. Direct response campaigns work to drive sales or specific user actions, like coupon downloads.

It is important to build strong brand recognition prior to focusing on a sales-driven media approach.

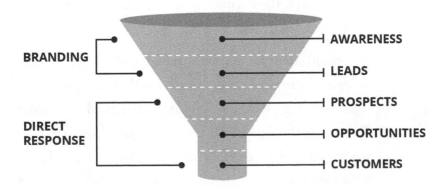

Source: Women's Marketing
Understanding Media Metrics and Analytics Webinar 2015

As you can see in the graphic, direct branding commercials, online videos, Amazon product videos, etc. seek to create awareness, education, credibility, conversion, and sales, whereas brand advertising stops at the first step, creating awareness. If you are getting people interested in your product, why not give them the opportunity to buy?

A great example of a powerful direct branding campaign would be the thirty-second commercials that GoPro made for their signature product that launched in 2011. Thirty-second spots are traditionally a length used only for big brand spots, like a Coca Cola ads, because direct response spots always work better with a longer format. But GoPro created a commercial that looked like a brand commercial with high production quality. The commercial opened with their brand logo, and at the end of it they said, "Go to our website. Someone will win one of everything we make every day." This spot was actually driving a specific response—and it worked. Viewers went to the site and registered, giving their names and email addresses in order to qualify for that contest. This was brilliant because:

- they successfully drove consumers to their site;

- they captured their names and email addresses and built their customer database;

- they could later take that information and remarket to that database every time they came out with a new product or video, sending information to those interested consumers. Then, once these potential customers got on the site, there was a showcase of all kinds of cool video content. People would share it with their friends, creating a viral aspect to the marketing, promoting the product even further and creating a foundation of word of mouth and community building;

- they immediately captured massive intel of user profiles of age, location, gender, and so on; and,

- most importantly, people could purchase the product directly, generating sales.

GoPro's 2013 holiday campaign included retail tags at the end of the commercial. Their chief retailer was Best Buy, so we added a tag saying, "Available at Best Buy," which was a strategic way to get the retail buyer to list the product. Shoppers want instant gratification: if they see something they like, they want it now. By creating this type of advertising, you're giving people the opportunity to do that. The strategy outlined above worked extremely well, and GoPro revenue grew to over $1 billion in sales in seven short years.

Retail tagging like this gives people the opportunity to know where to buy the product you're selling at brick-and-mortar retailers. This generates measurable revenue that you can use to fund your ad budget, which is the most important distinction between direct branding and pure brand advertising. Once you've educated the consumer and gotten them excited about your product, it's common sense to give them a simple way to purchase it.

Technology has changed the delivery of what we call the "command to purchase" or "call to action." Never forget: always ask for the order. Brand building key number five: direct branding; give the consumer a direct method to respond to your advertising and purchase your product by including your website address, toll-free number, or a number they can text for more information. In traditional brand or product marketing, there's a strategy to sell, but it's not based on asking for the order in an overt manner. Luxury and brand positioning advertising's goal is to originate, bolster, and support the brand legacy and the brand message, creating brand awareness. For instance, you can open up *Vanity Fair* and see a dazzling photo of a jar of skincare from Clinique, or perhaps a photo featuring a De Beers diamond ring; these ads never directly ask you for the order. You need to Google to discover more information, taking several steps before being able to order. They're creating the glamour and the sexiness of the brand through this imagery. Prestige products typically take this route: if you look at a picture of coffee from a Nespresso advertisement, it's beautiful and sumptuous; the foam is practically levitating off the cup. It creates desire, intimating that this product is going to make your life better.

> *Never forget: always ask for the order. Brand building key number five: direct branding; give the consumer a direct method to respond to your advertising and purchase your product by including your website address, toll-free number, or a number they can text for more information.*

In contrast, with direct response advertising, you're showing a website, text code, or an 800-number, creating a path to buying the product immediately. You're asking the consumer to place an order. An ad of this kind will also typically include some motivation for you to buy now, go online now, call now or text now—perhaps by including a free bonus, a certain discount, or other incentive. That response mechanism is a critical component we've always included in the ads we've built for consumer products.

If you're creating a luxury or prestige brand strategy and you have a very large budget to create and support your merchandise story, you can live in that rarified world of "image only" marketing. If you are launching a new product and working with limited capital, are beholden to your investors and shareholders, and you've got a sales plan you need to meet, then you need sales and income right away.

Luxury brands are those that cultivate experience over a longer timeline—and invest a great deal of money to do so—but new products and start-up companies don't generally have pockets that deep. Direct response allows you to build your brand while you're creating a revenue stream, and you don't need millions of dollars to do it. Branding and selling do not have to be mutually exclusive events.

Don't Forget that the Ultimate Purpose of Advertising is to Sell.

What's happened to a lot of brand advertising is that its creators have become too cute, pushing the envelope in pursuit of awards. They've gotten away from the purpose of advertising, which is basically to sell the product. There are a lot of examples of this, and they've been expensive failures for the companies that ran them. Remember the sock puppet that Pets.com used in its ads? They spent millions of dollars on advertising, but they didn't sell anything. They went from a high-profile, brand-only marketing campaign in 1998—spending millions of dollars—to closing their doors in 2000, one of the most noteworthy failures of the dotcom boom. Where might they be now if they had used direct branding to drive consumers to their site to generate sales instead? Pure branding agencies do not know how to do this and you can see the results.

If you're a small or a new business, you can't afford those kinds of unforced errors. Branding has to reflect the culture it lives in, and our culture is all about instant gratification.

Television was a big driver of this. Take the TV dinner, introduced in 1953. It allowed us to have a fully cooked meal that we simply had to reheat, so we could sit in front of the television, be entertained, and watch advertising. Instant mashed potatoes are another great example. Preparation is minimal; consumers were only required to boil water, add butter, and it was ready. In a "right now" culture, it's a strategic luxury to simply run brand advertising without a call to action (CTA). On Comcast, the screen overlay for the Home Shopping Network shows a "buy it now" button that lets consumers make a purchase by pushing the "okay" button on the remote, which is billed through their Comcast account. These kinds of shopping experiences are only going to become more ubiquitous as smart phones make it even easier to shop wherever you are, whenever you like. When consumers see something they want, they want it now, and they expect to get it same day in major markets or within two business days in the suburbs, free shipping included.

Another good example is how Instacart is using technology to make the grocery shopping experience seamless and headache-free. Instacart, the modern version of calling up the local deli down the street or the quick mart and saying, "I need a pound of sliced turkey and some potato salad," and having someone deliver it to your door in a couple of hours or when you tell them you want it delivered. Delivery service has existed for a long time of course, but the new tech has pushed its usage and acceptance as a service product into turbo speed. To reach today's busy consumer, you've got to offer them this kind of high-response, immediate option.

If you're not operating your business at this caliber, somebody else will be.

Direct response is typically perceived as infomercials and product marketing—short term, one-off products whose marketers are looking for a quick buck and then they're off to the next product. The problem with that is there's often no long-term strategy for customer acquisition, retention, relationship building, and brand awareness. In today's pavilion of sales and marketing, the wide range of platforms where consumers can shop reaches much further out than the old-style infomercial "shoot it and sell it" school of thought.

The point we're hammering across to you in this book is that every occasion in which the consumer interacts with your product and brand—whether that's via word of mouth, online reviews, seeing it in a friend's home, at a store, a digital platform, or on a late-night talk show—is just a wider form of sales conversation.

> *Every occasion in which the consumer interacts with your product and brand—whether that's via word of mouth, online reviews, seeing it in a friend's home, at a store, a digital platform, or on a late-night talk show—is just a wider form of sales conversation.*

Why Not Combine the Two?

So, what's the next logical step in the evolution of advertising? Brand response, which is long-term, strategic, and measurable. Many startups don't have the budget for big brand ad campaigns but can opt instead for what we call a "test and roll program." You can test Google Ad Words, or Facebook ads, or email marketing. You can test radio, TV ads, or Amazon and clearly see where you're getting responses. There are so many ways to interact with consumers and analytics to check the results of your expenditures. If you spent $100 over here, how much measurable revenue did that create? The idea is to measure back from the response standpoint all of the sales that have been created from the advertising, so you can allocate your resources to the kind of ad that was the most successful. The goal is to always break even or make money on your advertising in an immediate and measurable way.

Let's say you've got $10,000 allocated for ads. You've gotten orders from online, orders from your 800-number, and orders from Amazon. All of a sudden, the revenue that you've generated is twice the amount you've spent on advertising, because you have instant feedback and are able to measure the results. For every dollar of advertising spending, you're getting two back in return. Doesn't it make sense to put that money back on TV to create more sales? At the same time that you're creating more sales, you're also creating more brand awareness of your product or service. This simple concept is the powerful marketing secret behind the creation of dozens of our existing brands and sales revenue that can easily run into the hundreds of millions of dollars, and even reach a billion.

We were pioneers in this area, as we have been using the direct branding approach since 1990 and it's still relatively underutilized. If you took the number of companies in the country right now that are doing some type of brand response advertising, it's a tiny percentage versus all of the other companies that are doing strict, traditional brand advertising only. Why? Most advertising agencies don't understand the basics of direct response marketing, so they stick to what they know to the detriment of their clients' business welfare. Our philosophy is that more companies should market their products and services with some type of response mechanism in the advertising because it's been proven effective over and over again. It's a measurable, revenue-generating, brand-building blueprint for success within reach of almost any company trying to sell their products or services in today's marketplace.

The Momentus Golf Story

Jim Sorenson was a golf instructor who wanted to help his students improve their swing. He started experimenting with different aids that could help "groove their swing." Initially he had his students practice with a piece of rebar (a heavy length of steel used to reinforce concrete) and found that it did in fact improve their game. He reconfigured the rebar slightly to make it look more like a golf club and painted it yellow. He started a company around this one simple product, which he called Momentus Golf. We orchestrated the brand response advertising for the Momentus Swing Trainer, focusing on how it could improve a player's game. If you can promise a golfer a new item or technique that will shave a few strokes from their handicap, you will have an instant customer. We did this by showing ordinary golfers using the Momentus swing trainer and how it improved the golf score of each person that used it. Professional golfer Fred Funk hosted the infomercial, and we had a testimonial from David Duval, who had just won the British Open. Sales took off! The revenue that was generated was put back into the advertising campaign, and Jim was able to build a new golf brand and a $30 million company, just by using our simple brand response techniques—the same ones we are sharing in this book.

What separates brand response ads from traditional brand ads is the lack of accountability. This lack of accountability is great for the agency, but terrible for the client. The agency will show you dazzling impressions and reach, based on Nielsen ratings—a service used to measure potential viewers—and drives advertising rates for the programming where your ad is running. Traditional brand ads win awards for creativity, not sales revenue. Which would you rather have? We can measure and trace every dollar spent on advertising and the sales that are created through it. Obviously this is attractive to companies, because they like to see exactly what their return on investment (ROI) is. You've probably heard the famous quote from John Wanamaker: "Half the money I spend on advertising is wasted. I just don't know which half." Brand response advertising solves that problem, because you know how every dollar you spend is impacting your sales.

The days of retailers driving your sales with their advertising are done. The retailers rely on your advertising message, content, materials, and assets to drive the brand. The fact that they have a portal or a place to put your product to sell is the benefit of your relationship to them as a vendor, but they need you to drive shoppers into their doors and onto their website. Brand response advertising has been proven over and over again as the best way to do this.

Additionally, many brands formerly sold by these big retailers are leaving traditional stores and focusing on their own branded stores and their own e-commerce. This allows them to do two things: to control their pricing and control their brand message. They are not stuck inside the four walls of a retail environment going head-to-head against competitors trying to sell the same kinds of merchandise. These brands want shoppers to come into their environment where they can control their experience completely.

Your Branding Should Build a Community.

How can you turn a customer into a brand ambassador? You achieve this by creating a tribe a customer wants to be a part of. Smart sellers miss no opportunity to create the experience of belonging for their customers; from the handwritten thank-you card that's shipped with the product, to the follow-up email with a personalized "We hope you love it" message, you're building brand community.

Take as an example the Swell water bottle. We're a very water-conscious society these days, evidenced by the fact that practically all of us carry a bottle of water in our cars, purses, or briefcases. Swell has capitalized on this by bringing a tremendous amount of personalization to the market. You pick the bottle that matches you. They're constantly creating capsule collections, which are limited editions. When you choose one of these, it tells the world who you are. That particular bottle and the way that it's designed is a statement that reflects your personality. Why does this strategy work? Our need for affirmation—when the consumer opens her beautiful Swell package and it's got a little chamois holder she can put her bottle in to keep it clean, it endorses her decision-making that she made the right choice. It's an affirmation. Everyone who sees it says, "Oh, that's so cool. Where did you get it?" The customer tells them, and hence, becomes a "brand ambassador." She loves the attention, she's part of the Swell tribe, and she has the bottle to prove it.

The Downside? That Community Can Also Turn on a Product.

Thanks to the Internet, a bad review can go viral in seconds, doing your brand enormous damage. The empowerment of opinion has changed the way that consumers look at a product. The engagement a consumer has with your brand and your product is immediate and much more impactful than it was five or ten years ago. Ten years ago if you loved a product enough to make the effort, you'd write a thank-you letter to the president of the company. Now all the consumer has to do is to go online. Most people are happy to log on and give a review—but those aren't always going to be positive, because everyone loves to be a critic. If they think your product is crap, they'll say so online. So make sure it isn't.

Good social media is critical. Social is word of mouth. It's friends. It's building community and creating an army of brand ambassadors, because the good reviews of your loyal community can help balance the bad ones. Monitor and manage customer reviews, but don't sanitize them. If all your reviews are five stars it is not believable, and you lose the hard-fought campaign for credibility, because customers expect there to be some less-than-glowing appraisals.

Mobile devices are the gateway, because mobile is outpacing everything in terms of search and purchasing. And remember—your brand is going to be looked at globally. It doesn't matter if you're only selling it in Kansas City because that's where you live. If you're on the Internet, it's a global window.

Summary

General or brand advertising creates awareness for your brand, while good direct response advertising educates, establishes credibility, and drives conversion and sales. If you are a small business or are launching a new product with a limited budget you can compete with the big guys with direct brand advertising. Remember, always give the consumer a direct way to order your product or service.

CHAPTER THREE

The Power of Positioning

"Customers have to know and feel the brand as an experience that serves their individual needs. It has to be a total and on-going immersion in satisfaction that includes everything from packaging to point of purchase, repurchase, and after-the-sale service and communication."

—Les Wunderman, *Being Direct: Making Advertising Pay*

Next up is brand building key number two: positioning, or finding a category that you can dominate. In a previous chapter we referenced a book called the *Blue Ocean Strategy*. If you've never read it, you should, but we'll save you the time by sharing its core point: Zig when everybody else is zagging. It's about finding a category that you can dominate. The

> **Brand building key number two: positioning, or finding a category that you can dominate.**

book's title refers to the need to leave the safety of well-known waters where all your competitors are fishing and head out into uncharted seas where no one else ventures. You want to head for open territory where nobody else thinks (or dares) to go. That is where you want your brand to be to have the best chance of success.

RICK:

66 How you choose to position your brand can make or break it—and sometimes simply changing how your product is positioned can turn it from a failure into a success. We talked earlier about the George Foreman Grill, the phoenix that rose from the ashes of the defunct Fajita Express. We didn't substantially change the product, but we did change its positioning from a gadget for making tacos to a tool to help you enjoy the grilled meats you love while cutting fat and eating healthier. Just from that one positioning change, the George Foreman Grill went on to sell more than any other product in housewares history. Similarly, we repositioned the Juiceman from a small appliance to focusing on the benefits of the juice from the machine, which made all the difference. There are many other examples of how simple repositioning brought a product back from the dead. 99

BARB:

66 In 2004, I was working for a company that is a market leader in health and wellness. They had a cool product that used a system of colored LED lights to create an atmosphere of tranquility in a room. The product used a speaker input jack to pick up the tempo of the music, and the tempo of the lights would change according to the

music. But it hadn't taken off—consumers just weren't interested. This was in the early days of the iPod, and as I looked at the product, I asked, "Why can't this work with my iPod?" I brought my iPod in to show my new colleagues, who didn't know what I was talking about. At that time, there was only one dedicated iPod speaker system on the market: Altec Lansing.

The company made an appointment to visit Apple's execs in Cupertino, where they had a fantastic meeting and got the license for their nine-pin connector. They re-launched it as an iPod accessory, and labeled it as such. Suddenly, a product that consumers had not been interested in was raking in serious revenue. The executive who created this lighting/music system was initially very resistant to the idea of repositioning it within the electronics vertical. Its success shifted his focus and now his business is largely in the consumer electronics vertical.

If your product is not resonating with consumers because your vision is limiting the use of the product, be open to repositioning your goods or services in order to meet contemporary user demand. We know people who use Uber as a taxi service, but we also know people who use it as a delivery service for food. Look at what your product or service is or does: how can it be repurposed or regenerated to be more useful/hip/in sync with other, more successful products, or fulfill an unmet need? 🙾

Failure to Reposition Can Be Fatal.

Another company with which we were associated manufactured supplements, and had created a proprietary supplement for women intended to balance hormones. Interestingly, "menopause" and "peri-menopause" are words which many avoid saying out loud, yet contextually they're among the most searched terms on the Internet. Women are looking for information on the symptoms they're experiencing to both educate themselves and discuss with their doctors. That's why it was amazing to us that one of the team members who was managing this product flatly refused to let us use the word "menopause" in any marketing. Even in SEO! In fact, if you mentioned menopause in a meeting, you ran the risk of getting kicked off the team. The really odd part is that the founder wanted to pitch this product to younger women in their twenties and early thirties and rejected any kind of emotive terms in discussing the product, opting to go instead for a highly scientific tone rather than hitting those emotional targets. The consumers voted and they weren't interested. The product never got beyond a very narrow niche market. Founder's syndrome claimed another victim, but had they chosen to listen to the customers, rather than ignoring them, they may have had a dynamic, revenue producing launch.

> *Instead of trying to control consumers' behavioral response, let the consumer's insights and behaviors decide what they want to do with your product and you'll get more buyers.*

Instead of trying to control consumers' behavioral response, let the consumer's insights and behaviors decide what they want to do with your product and you'll get more buyers. If your customer finds a better, smarter use for your product than you had imagined, embrace it! A client we worked with was a snack manufacturer who decided to make a small appliance they wanted the consumers to use with their food product and only their product.

When you take that hardline stance, you immediately limit yourself to a smaller slice of market share. (People will do crazy things with products—we had an electric sandwich maker that a hockey player decided was the perfect device to use to warm up his hockey sticks. He took a saw and cut out part of the product so that he could put the hockey stick in there and warm it up.) Certainly, when it comes to a food product that you buy at the grocery store, if it's within the same category, chances are the consumer is going to assume they can use whatever brand they want in the product—and you can't stop them from "off label" use.

Inventor's syndrome is a related type of marketing myopia to founder's syndrome that can prevent you from seeing your product's potential or its limitations. Just as every mother's child is above average, every inventor's brainchild is a genius creation. That's why you have folks lining up to go on Shark Tank with their inventions, each of them certain that their baby is going to make them millions. Sometimes they can't see the forest through the trees. Rejuvenique, which we talked about earlier, had that hockey mask-like appearance. Women were willing to put it on, but the product's visual was relentlessly mocked. The inventors didn't want to hear it.

Another product undone by inventor's syndrome was a vacuum sealer for food. The owners of the company insisted on calling it food storage. Because the vendor decided the product was a storage item (even though it was a sealer), the naming classification meant that the vacuum sealer buyer at the retailer could not buy the product and merchandise it where it belonged and where consumers would know to look for vacuum sealers being sold. The product owner then had to go to the storage buyer because it says "storage" all over the packaging. Lastly, the existing vendors in the storage category effectively took up all of the shelf space and there was no room to add these goods to the product selection on the floor. Simple things can get complicated when we refuse to get out of our own way.

Lesson learned? Make sure that you do your research at retail before you name or categorize your new product. Go to mass-market retailers, go to department stores and walk their floors and see where the product is. Search Amazon and Google. Put your ego out of the equation and assess the competitive landscape. While you're at it, go visit a few closeout stores and pay attention to what you see on the shelf.

SWOT Analysis: Strength, Weaknesses, Opportunities, and Threats

Doing a proper SWOT analysis of your product (determining its strengths, weaknesses, opportunities, and threats) is a critical step before you begin branding. Today if you walk into Bed Bath & Beyond, you'll see two major versions of the vacuum storage product: (1) the original product, and (2) the product produced by consumer package goods (CPG) companies, which are similar and in the exact same color as those this former client is selling. That creates visual confusion for the customer: *What am I getting? What does it do?* People don't dependably read packaging, so that first impression your product makes when the consumer sees the packaging or the product is what's really critical. Now they're seeing different brands of different products that look confusingly similar but are functionally very different. Your product gets lost in the clutter on the shelf. That's why a SWOT analysis is invaluable.

Do your homework. See what's out there. What does your product look like? What does it smell like? What does it taste like? What does it retail for? How is it being marketed? Why is it different?

What do you want to say to the consumer? If it is a new product category, ask yourself why nobody has launched it before. Maybe it *has* been done before, but it proved to be a bad category or product idea.

Today you might go to the retail buyer with that product but the buyer will say, "Hey, I'm not taking those goods. I've got two others on my shelf right now. They're not moving." Your product might be the best thing in the world. It could really light its category on fire, but the buyer's got two other products like it sitting there taking up shelf space and not producing turn. It goes back always to the money: What's the revenue stream? Is it working or not working?

Your consumer may go to a store to see a product in person, but she's going to go home and buy it online with free shipping, no tax, free returns, and a ninety-day guarantee. This is called "showrooming," because the retailer has effectively become the showroom. This paradigm shift in how the consumer is shopping has radically changed the face of retail, and retail trend data on brick-and-mortar stores shows that many are closing because of online sales and changing consumer behavior. Major retailers closed over three thousand stores in 2017, including Kmart, Sears, Bebe, Rue21, JC Penny's, Macy's, Abercrombie & Fitch, Guess, Crocs, the Limited, Wet Seal, American Apparel, BCBG, Payless Shoesource, GameStop, RadioShack, Staples, CVS, Gander Mountain, Toys"R"Us, and Babies"R"Us.[3]

---

3   Mike Timmermann, "These Major Retailers Have Closed More than 5,000 Stores in 2017," Clark.com, Dec. 13, 2017, https://clark.com/shopping-retail/major-retailers-closing-2017/.

How Do You Look, and What Does Your Package Say to the Consumer?

In a competitive marketplace, it doesn't matter if you're selling gym shoes or dancing lessons; how you wrap the package around your product or service creates a brand legend.[4] Athletic shoes are a great example. Again, there's not really all that much differentiation in the actual product: There's a sole. There's a footpad. There are shoelaces or some type of a closure system. Many of these brands are produced in the same offshore factories. What matters is what the brand does to give that product personality. How is the brand creating a legend around that product? Just ask Nike.

When you're looking at your packaging, don't depend on your own judgment. Put it in the hands of people with no stake in the product, people who will be honest. Spend the money; do the anthropological testing. Get a sense of the user experience. Whatever feedback you get, listen to it. Is the type too small? Are the colors unappealing? Does it confuse the consumer, or appeal to them?

BARB

" I experienced a striking illustration of this when I was working at Wolfgang Puck Worldwide and met David Scully, formerly of Campbell's Soup and the then-owner of Wolfgang's soup company.

---

4   A legendary graphic designer, Tibor Kalman, wrote a *New York Times* piece many years ago that's a classic—serving literally as a tutorial on the power of graphic communications and the messages it sends. His subject: spaghetti sauce in a jar, and the messaging that the label telegraphs to the consumer. His brand-by-brand analysis of the graphics, typefaces, colors, and probable buyers of spaghetti sauce is epic. It's a brilliant breakdown that really underscores the impact of packaging—highly recommended reading.

We were at a Publix market in Florida for a Wolfgang Puck event, upstairs in an open loft-like mezzanine from which could be seen the entire floor of the grocery store. He pointed down and asked, "What are the first things you see in those two aisles?"

The first, immediate, nano-second impression I spotted from that raised level was the orange/red packaging of Tide detergent, and the red of Campbell's Soup. For me, this really underscored the importance of seeing what your competition looks like on the retail floor. The eye drives you to the destination in the shopping aisle. Once the consumer is there, how does your brand communicate with the eye? **"**

Make Sure You're Not Sending Customers to Your Competitors.

When we were marketing products directly to the consumer on television, even though we were selling directly to the consumer from the ad, it was also driving retail sales. We were creating product awareness, driving people into the stores to buy—but we discovered that connection almost by accident.

Back in the early '90s, when we were first promoting Juiceman, we were strictly a direct to consumer (D2C) company, selling via the 800-number or direct mail because e-commerce hadn't been invented yet. But a major housewares magazine ran a big story about how the Juiceman advertising was actually pushing Braun and Krups juicers at retail, because Juiceman wasn't available in retail. That was the first time that we made the connection between what we were doing from a direct response advertising standpoint and the effect it was having on other distribution channels. We'd run our advertising and get people to come out to a free seminar and the juicers selling at retail—the Brauns and the Krups—would start flying off the shelves. Talk about unintended consequences. That was when we realized that our D2C campaigns could also push retail sales. Over the last twenty years we put that insight to use building a lot of the big well-known brands we talk about in this book. Now when we spend our advertising dollars, we're looking at the immediate sales that are created from an 800-number, from the website or the landing page from Amazon, and from the brick-and-mortar retail sales.

This is what's called omni-channel marketing/sales. It could be online. It could be through mobile, or via SMS. It could be on TV, radio, or print—all types of media. That's how you reach your consumer—by being where they are, with what they want, when they want to buy it. Don't fail to meet them there, because they'll go to your competitor for the next best thing if you do. If you're going to launch a product, be really clear from the get-go what your goals are. If you decide a year and a half into your campaign development you don't want to go to retail, and everybody has been working on a campaign that's driving toward retail, you've wasted a lot of money.

Reach your consumer by being where they are, with what they want, when they want to buy it. Don't fail to meet them there, because they'll go to your competitor for the next best thing if you do.

On the other hand, if you want to go to retail and the retailers say no, you have options today through e-commerce, Amazon, eBay, and other online market places. Again, *pay attention to the data*. One great thing about data driven marketing is the data doesn't lie.

The Takeaway? Do Your Homework.

Do the SWOT analysis: Walk the stores; look at websites. Go through your competitors' packaging, their positioning, and their advertising. See how they're trending out in the digital ecosystem. Learn by their mistakes. See what resonates for you and your product. Listen to people.

Don't try to force consumer behavior. We tell this to our clients all the time: Let the customer buy the product where they want to buy it, whether that's on TV, in retail, online, e-commerce, Amazon, or any other online store. Don't try to force them to buy at a certain place. Let the customer buy the product where they're most comfortable, and they'll reward you with greater sales.

SUMMARY

When getting ready to launch a new product or to re-launch an existing product, think about your positioning. Is it a new category that is open or an existing one that you can dominate? This holds true whether you are trying to sell a book on Amazon or launch the next great consumer product.

CHAPTER FOUR

- -

What's in a Name?

"Authentic brands don't emerge from marketing cubicles or advertising agencies. They emanate from everything the company does."
— Howard Schultz, former CEO of Starbucks

RICK:

We'll begin this chapter with a confession: when I was younger and more egotistical, I thought that I was so good at marketing that it didn't matter what the product name was. If it was marketed well, I could overcome that. Subsequent experience and the wisdom that comes with it has changed my mind: a good name is significantly helpful to building your brand, positioning your brand, and ultimately gaining the thing you want, which is customer acceptance.

So how do you come up with a name? You may think this is an easy process—just sit around and brainstorm until something clicks—but there's more to consider than you might initially have considered. Will your name mean something different (and potentially offensive) in another language, or to another culture? Is it already in use somewhere for another product? Does a bigger company that can afford to outbid you for search results own it? Back in the '80s and early '90s pre-Internet, you had to go to a patent and trademark lawyer and pay a lot of money to get a name search done, whereas now you have the ability to do most of that yourself and for free online.

If you've come up with a name you think works, your first move should be to Google it to check for trademark clearance and registration and see where the marketing landmines are (i.e., who else is using it, and in what territory they're using it). If you want a global product and your name is being used by a company in Europe, you're going to put a lot of effort to build a brand around a mark you won't be able to use in that territory—or wind up paying a lot of money for the rights to it. Vet, vet, vet—or be prepared to pay the price. 〞

HOW DO EXPERTS COME UP WITH A NAME?

- We often begin our naming process with a computer program called Visual Thesaurus that, like its name suggests, provides alternative words or terms that convey a similar feeling, thought, or expression.

- They ask themselves what their brand stands for. Does this product have a feminine, masculine, or gender-neutral personality? Gorilla Glue is an example of a very masculine-driven product.

- They consider if the logo will need to be a form factor in the industrial design. It's important to consider how your logo will look within the actual design of your product. Method Soap is a great example of getting this right; the bottle is in the shape of a droplet, giving the logo and identity an intuitive synchronicity. The form factor of the actual product is its packaging, and their logo works within that as a structure, creating a memorable shopping and usage experience with the name.

The Best Names are Short, Sweet, and Memorable.

Look at how many of the successful products we have worked with have names with just two syllables—Juiceman, Breadman, GoPro, Space Bags, and Rug Doctor to name just a few. Serendipity has played a big part in more than a few successful names, though of course you can't count on luck!

BARB:

Two examples of names that benefitted from being ahead of their times: First, I worked on a simple, convenience-driven product for Salton in the 1990s, a desktop appliance initially called the Mug Warmer, which did exactly what the name suggests; very succinct, but not inspired. Looking for a better name, our team decided upon, "the Hot Spot." Hot Spot was a trademark Salton had for its hot trays. The section of the tray with an extra-hot area was called the Hot Spot, and at this point we'd had the trademark for many, many years.

Again, this was the 1990s, so we were very much pre-Internet. However, in the second year after the renaming, WiFi hotspots started popping up all over, notably at Starbuckses in collaboration with T-Mobile. Suddenly there was a linkage between the name of this product that was about keeping your coffee hot at your desk and this hip, new technology associated in the public's mind with Starbucks, and it became a product language that had a more current, relevant meaning. Another example of serendipity was a Salton ice cream maker we named the "Big Chill," a non-electric, hand-crank, "frozen dessert maker." This was also the name of a popular movie that came out around the same time.

Today an entertainment company would take immediate care to lock down naming rights across multiple categories, and this is where licensing would drive your naming strategies. **"**

RICK

" The other way luck can work is in the bad direction—as with the bathroom tub and tile cleaner, Kaboom. Its makers wanted a name that sounded powerful, and Kaboom fit the bill. Unfortunately, they were just finishing up the pre-launch process when 9/11 happened. They ended up delaying the product's debut for several months. Ultimately, they were able to weather it and turn it into a successful brand that is still widely distributed on store shelves, but it was certainly less than an ideal launch. **"**

BARB:

" A few years back, I was on a hike with the founder of a new supplement company, and we were kicking around names for his brand. He knew he wanted the name to tell the product story and to encourage daily use by consumers—so the name Daily Wellness popped up. This name invites consumers to think of their health as a daily commitment, and the use of Wellness as a goal terminology worked. The brand name stuck and the products are embraced by consumers and still selling very well today. You can find their products in many GNC stores nationwide.

But beware: the perfect name sometimes has less than perfect associations. Take the Flush and Shut, a problem-solution mechanism, created by a gentleman to quietly put the seat down on a toilet after use. He put a great deal of time and effort into a dampening system so that the seat didn't slam down and awaken his wife in the middle of the night. The product also solved the problem of the "three a.m. surprise" many of us have if someone in the house leaves the seat up, and the bathroom is dark, etc.

The name spoke directly and clearly to what the product did. When we made an infomercial for it, however, our inbound phone lines were inundated with crank calls. Flush and Shut was a really clever device, but it cost us a fortune on the marketing side to have operators answering crank calls all day. The product couldn't sustain nor survive the downside of its name associations. "

A Name Change Can Make all the Difference in a Product's Success.

RICK:

" I happened to see a story on *60 Minutes* about a guy who had developed a unique system for teaching kids how to do mathematics. The name of his program was Mike's Math. After the episode aired on *60 Minutes*, we reached out to Mike and started to help him with his marketing. I knew we could turn it into a much more successful business, but Mike's Math was not the best name, even though it carried the name of its founder, Mike Byster. Mike was the inventor and spokesperson, and he wanted to keep his product name because he already had customers and some traction, plus the exposure of being on *60 Minutes*, but we had to roll it out into something that would define the product's mission. We knew this had the potential to be big, so we brought in Joel Appel, one of the original founders of OxiClean, to help with financing on this project. We went through a naming process using a firm in Seattle called Heckler, which is famous for creating the Starbucks logo. They came up with the name Brainetics, this new name created a brand umbrella for a business that went from a little Mom-and-Pop operation to doing millions of dollars in sales. Why did the name Brainetics work? Simply because it sounded more modern and scientific; it gave the brand more legitimacy, though the product itself was unchanged.

Another product we worked on was the furniture polish Orange Glo. This product was also part of the OxiClean family of products. Consumers were familiar with Lemon Pledge and furniture polish products that were, by and large, lemon-scented (before Orange Glo came into the market). Their unique selling proposition (USP) was the orange peel oil in their product, and its distinctive scent and cleaning abilities differentiated it from other products in the market. In the initial advertising, we showed a beautiful tree full of oranges that would graphically change into the bottle Orange Glo furniture spray, which brought to mind the pleasant smell and natural freshness of the product.

Remember, to be successful in building your brand, you must differentiate your product from all the other competitors in the marketplace. Otherwise, like we talked about when we discussed the first brand building key—your unique selling proposition—you are just a commodity. 🙶

Does Your Product Come with a Personality Attached?

Some successful products have a personality that comes with their names—like the Breadman, the Juiceman, or the Rug Doctor. Retailers can use actual names to give their products a special personality and niche in the marketplace—even at stores generally better known for low prices than for high style. Look at the success that Target has had since the late '90s with its capsule collections of various designer lines—clothes by Missoni and the housewares lines created by Phillip Starck or Michael Graves, for instance. All of the capsule collections are rolled out on a limited time basis, which creates urgency. It was certainly very successful and brought in a tremendous amount of prestige and free PR for Target.

Beware of Founderitis

We've talked about the perils of founderitis (founder's syndrome), or the tendency of inventors or business founders to have tunnel vision when it comes to their idea, in previous chapters. This can happen with naming, too: the inventor comes up with what they see as the perfect name and refuses to listen to anyone who suggests otherwise.

If you are naming a product, don't necessarily go with your first impulse; ask others for their input and listen to the naysayers who aren't as in love with it as you are. They may be on to something that your personal attachment to the product is preventing you from hearing. We've talked about culture clashes in naming products, but also remember to test your name across genders, because what resonates with one may be meaningless or offensive to another.

Recently, we witnessed some inventors create a really terrific product. They invested in tooling, factory setup, compliance costs, and photo shoots. But they didn't build a brand name that would resonate with the audience. They created a brand name and product name hierarchy that *they* loved and thought was funny, but most consumers didn't relate to. The product is called the G-spout and is used for pouring hot grease out of pans.

In fact, the product name is so counter to the actual use of the product, especially in the USA, that it leads to more than a little confusion regarding its purpose to consumers. Unfortunately, this wonderful product, which really is a useful food preparation tool, is saddled with a name that turns many people off. The name says nothing that's helpful or attractive to a potential consumer; it doesn't describe the product or give it an identity that's congruent in any way with what it does. When we were showing the product around to people, their response was uniformly, "Why do they call it this?" This is a case where the inventor and founder overrode our objections and stayed with their original name. There is no doubt in our minds that this seriously affected overall sales of the product.

Leave your customers with great impressions of a brand name, look, and feel that encourages buy-in, not turn off. That's when that one naysayer's comment may become useful. If somebody shrugs and says, "I don't get it," then in all likelihood he's not going to be the only one who doesn't get it. Brand building key number four: always listen to customer feedback. It's hard enough to launch a product and build a great brand. Why get off to a bad start with a poor name and watch your product struggle to overcome it?

> *Brand building key number four: always listen to customer feedback.*

Think of the story of the *Emperor's New Clothes*: that naysayer just may be the honest person that says, "But you don't have anything on." It hurts to hear that, but you've already invested so much into bringing your product to market; don't risk it all at this stage simply out of pride or misplaced ego.

A FOUNDER'S CHECKLIST FOR FOOLPROOF PRODUCT NAMING:

- Start by asking your team, friends, and family to independently suggest names because you know what happens when you get the whole group in a room: everybody starts feeding on the one name. You want to encourage as much spontaneous, uninfluenced creativity and originality as possible.

- Go to the United States Patent and Trademark office's website and to Google and do a search and see if anyone else is using your name. Do not skip this step, even if you're convinced that your name is so specific and unusual that nobody could have come up with it before.

- If there is another product with the identical or a similar name, think about the long-term applications of the name in terms of your advertising spend, your advertising plan, and your digital advertising deployment. "Likelihood of confusion" is a trademark registration test that you've got to pass, even across product categories and verticals.

- How will the next generation or line extension products fit within the brand name hierarchy? Are you going to call it the Super Duper Plus, the Super Duper Pro, the Super Duper XXL, or the Super Duper Designer? How do you extend the brand?

- Consider what the brand looks like in the sense of its graphic identity. As its identity is formed, does that identity fit the product's position? We've seen people use fonts and photography that are more down market than an elevated brand would require.

- Go to the store and observe the area in which your product will be displayed. Look at what your competitors are doing to get their messaging and service across. How do you stack up? Visually weak logos don't help anybody. When you're walking down an aisle at the store and you've got twenty-four feet of product, where does the eye go?

- Not every product goes straight to brick-and-mortar, so alternately, if the product is going to launch on e-commerce, what will your product look like online?

- What's your content delivery, and how robust is your content? Do you have all of the necessary bells and whistles in your tool chest? When the buyer says, "We're going to put you online," you've got to have all of those assets put together to build your brand the best possible way. Is your imagery beautiful, or does it fall flat? Does it meet the technical specs the retailers will need?

- Understand the cost and operational impact of trademark protection. Getting your patent is only the first step. Are you prepared to defend your patent and defend your trademark?

- If you are manufacturing goods offshore, do you need trademark protection elsewhere, and can you and your company cover the cost?

Brand names that we've worked on are all popular and well-known names now, but even when they were first launched, they were cool-sounding names that rolled of the tongue and helped make you want to learn more.

Summary

Make sure your name catches not only consumers' eyes, but also their imaginations. Once you find a name that you like, remember to research, clear it for use, and always vet, vet, vet!

CHAPTER FIVE

Deliver Value

"The key is to set realistic customer expectations, and then not to just meet them, but to exceed them— preferably in unexpected and helpful ways."

—Richard Branson, founder, Virgin Group

One of the biggest mistakes we often see made in marketing is over-promising and under-delivering. Marketers build up an expectation of what the consumer is going to get but let them down when the product doesn't live up its marketing claims. Especially in the direct-to-consumer marketing field, unscrupulous marketers have made a lot of money by making extravagant promises on which the product can't deliver. Yes, you can sell a lot of products very rapidly that way, but if people aren't happy with what they get, word spreads very quickly, your sales will dwindle, and your product cycle will be short lived. This is the opposite of what we are looking to accomplish when we are trying to create a brand.

What we'd suggest as a much more successful brand-building alternative is to *under*-promise and *over*-deliver—brand building key number three. This means when you order a product online, through TV, or find it at a retail store, you are pleasantly surprised by the product being even better than you'd hoped. That creates a good feeling about the brand—a positive impression your consumer is more likely to want to share with others. That great word of mouth conversation will snowball, especially in today's social media environment, and you'll be on your way to building your brand and creating a stellar reputation for your company and product line.

> *What we'd suggest as a much more successful brand-building alternative is to under-promise and over-deliver—brand building key number three.*

BARB:

❝ You never forget your first experience as a consumer being seduced by an endorsement that didn't pay off. I vividly remember when, as a young girl, I persuaded my parents to buy me a bag of snacks, solely because my two favorite cartoon characters, Rocky and Bullwinkle, were shown on the bag. The incentive was that there was a special surprise collectible inside.

As a kid, I probably thought that somehow Rocky and Bullwinkle supervised this entire operation, ensuring that the surprise was packed inside and I was going to be blown away by this awesome gift.

Even so, convincing my parents to buy that bag of Dipsy Doodles was a challenging mission. When Mom and Dad allowed me to open the bag, it was an unforgettable unboxing moment of disappointment—no prize, no gift, nothing but chips. This was my very first experience with consumer disillusionment, albeit from a first grader's experience level. The value proposition or the closer on that sale was getting that coveted Rocky and Bullwinkle prize, and I'd been stiffed. My father sat down with me as I composed and mailed my first consumer complaint letter.

A few weeks later, an apology came in the mail with a whole package of the prizes. But even so, that initial disappointment is what I remember most about the experience, and that's as true for adults as it is for kids.

Unboxing counts! If you think it through and make it great, then you've made a long-lasting impression that tilts toward the positive. **" "**

WHEN YOU INTRODUCE A PRODUCT IN TODAY'S MARKETPLACE, YOU'VE GOT TO PUT YOURSELF IN YOUR CUSTOMER'S SHOES AND ASK:

- Does every touch point deliver? How is the consumer's experience—from the moment they purchase your product to when they first use it?

- Does it feed their senses on as many levels as possible? Does it surround them with pleasure? The sensory experience begins with the packaging. Fifteen years ago, a glossy box was the norm.

However, today many companies, especially in the electronics and cosmetics worlds, are using what we call a soft-touch coating. That means that the minute the consumer gets the product into their hands, they're getting a positive feeling.

• Does it feed their ego by making them feel they've made a smart decision?

Our Golden Rule of Branding is to always treat your customer the way you would like to be treated.

When we were selling the George Foreman Grill, we included at no extra charge a valuable recipe book, as well as a food spatula in the box. These were unexpected additions that made the customer feel good when they got the grill. When customers ordered the Juiceman, we not only included free recipes and a pairing knife and cutting board for cutting produce, we also included a cleaning brush and a juice pitcher so that when consumers received the Juiceman they had everything they needed to get started juicing and using our product right away. We made sure they received copies of a product newsletter and information on the anti-aging and immune boosting properties of fresh juice too; that underscored the fact that they'd made a wise decision. All these things were extras that built value and made the Juiceman juicer stand apart from a Krups or a Braun, which were basically being sold as an appliance and not a lifestyle product. That's a blueprint we've followed with almost every product we've marketed. Create a product lifestyle that resonates with consumers' emotive aspirations and give people more value than they are expecting.

When we marketed the Rug Doctor, we packaged it with specialty cleaning products like pet stain remover, red wine remover, spot and stain cleaner, and oxy-boost for deep carpet cleaning. It was about $80 worth of extra cleaning products, included free. That meant the consumer could start using the Rug Doctor machine the day he or she got it, without an extra trip to the store. That was real added value, and consumers' responses to it were overwhelmingly positive.

Don't Nickel and Dime Your Customer.

When you sell a core product, it's always wise to include the essential accessories as part of the main purchase. Too often companies decide that they're going to make a little extra money by selling those secondary products, and they get stingy when it comes to providing them to consumers as gifts with purchase. This is short-term thinking and not long-term brand building behavior. They see themselves selling these accessory products and getting rich, but what happens instead is consumers get annoyed and feel as though they've been ripped off. When you open the box, you expect your product to work. When you've got to go shopping before you can plug it in and use it, that's an irritation. An irritated customer might return your product, will probably speak badly about it, and definitely will not buy more from you.

Happy Customers Like to Spread the Good News.

The oldest form of marketing is positive word of mouth. This is enhanced in today's marketplace through social media. The happier consumers are, the more they talk about a product, and thanks to the amplifying effect of social media, that happiness is broadcast with a sense of urgency. Of course, if you're not delivering value, that gets around quickly, too. Part of building value is building a community of happy consumers, a fact that too many businesses selling on the Internet forget about, to their cost. Too often we see Internet marketers who are fixated solely on making the next sale when their first concern should be leaving a great impression on the customers they've got. Even if your follow-up product is in a different category than your initial offering, that positive brand experience the first time around will influence your customer to try your new product, because you've built connection and trust. If you're providing great customer service along with a great-looking product that really works and the customers know they can trust you, then they'll buy whatever it is you want to sell down the line. It is much easier and cheaper to sell to an existing customer than to constantly have to create new ones.

Equation for Success: Trust + Value + Messaging = Sales

"A brand is no longer what we tell the consumer it is—it is what consumers tell each other it is."

—Tim Cook, president of Apple

"This is what I make. Don't you want it?" The call of the information age is consumers asking, "This is what I need. Won't you make it?"

A product must create value for its consumers. It must satisfy consumers' unique differences, not their commonalities. The call of the industrial revolution was manufacturers saying, "This is what I make. Don't you want it?" The call of the information age is consumers asking, "This is what I need. Won't you make it?"

We're seeing the truth of this equation for success proved again and again by the marketplace triumphs of disruptive companies like the Dollar Shave Club or Harry's. In the old days, Gillette produced whatever they wanted to make and over-priced their products, then pushed them out to the consumer. Consumers got tired of that, so then along came the Dollar Shave Club, giving people a choice and delivering real value, and consumers embraced it. The company recently sold for about a billion dollars—that's a lot of razors.

But, sometimes a creator goes overboard in inventing a product so cutting edge and ahead of its time that consumers reject it.

BARB

In my first year at Salton, our chairman, David Sabin, decided that the company was going to make the first talking coffee maker. This was in 1986, before email, back when the fax machine was still considered cutting edge, having replacing the telex.

A group of very advanced automotive engineers from Detroit created a coffee maker that announced by voice to let you know that your coffee was ready. It wasn't exactly Alexa, Siri, or Google Home, but the operating system of the coffeemaker could speak four or five phrases. We took it to focus groups, expecting an overwhelmingly positive response. What we got was an overwhelming *NO!*

In 1986, women were vehemently opposed to talking coffee makers. Today's technology brings us multiple AI interfaces in our homes—Alexa, Siri, and Google Home, for instance. In 1986, people couldn't grasp the idea of having a Jetsons-like space age machine in their kitchens, and the product didn't fulfill a psychographic need. It didn't create value. It created an annoyance at that moment on the cultural timeline.

The Breadman, on the other hand, created a wonderfully rich sensory experience. You could certainly go to the market and buy a loaf of bread more easily—but the smell of baking bread is a potently delicious perfume, and customers responded to it with soulful love. A bread machine is really just a computer with a motor that bakes bread and does no more than you could do with a stand mixer and a pan in your oven. But this was an appliance that would deliver that functionality in a box. Plus, it created this beautiful visual stimulation of seeing the bread rise and bake, and the bread itself was excellent, so it fired on all cylinders for taste and texture. But it was the aroma that sealed the deal with consumers.

How we shaped this particular brand was by spending a lot of time asking what customers really wanted when it came to bread. What do they dream about? They dream about the fresh-baked ciabatta they'd had in Tuscany when they were on a trip in Italy ten years ago. The flavors and taste melted in their mouth; or they remembered when they were in Paris and they'd had this marvelous baguette that just couldn't be replicated. In the competitive marketplace, there were companies pushing bread machines that trimmed time off of the baking process, but the flavor, textures, and results just weren't up to par. And in developing the Breadman we were committed to making the best possible bread in the most appealing package. Getting those touch points right mattered—the artwork that's supported by the brand, the brand voice, the look and feel, and moreover the product that came out of that machine—because we wanted to do everything we could so that the whole package would please the customer. It was really the beginning of the movement toward community building in the home appliance business; in no time, our customers were swapping Breadman recipes and how-tos. In the early days of the Internet prior to Reddit, message boards and user groups developed opinion-led communities regarding products and they spread the word on Breadman. Yes, these were the pioneers of digital influencers.

Leon Dreimann, the president of Salton at that time, was a visionary, and he supported me to the extent that the company sent me to two professional-level artisan baking programs—one at the Dunwoody Institute in Minneapolis, and the second at the French Culinary Institute. Understanding the science of food, its ingredients, and how technology can drive the success of a recipe is invaluable. A special thanks to Leon for his perceptiveness, and for allowing me to advance our marketing by advancing the technology to create a prestige brand that owned the market.

I recently had the pleasure of working with the high caliber team at Johnsonville Sausage. Over a period of several years, they created an indoor grill for their sausages, driven by performance with their food product. While it was created to specifically work with Johnsonville Sausages and Brats, the results, each and every time, are outstanding and delicious.

Johnsonville's attention to detail and excellence—a hallmark of their brand equity on the food side—drove them to create a "hardware" product of equal performance values. Why? Because their brand legacy and their consumer community deserve that level of excellence. 🔊🔊

What do you need to build an engaged and loyal tribe of consumers around a good or great product? Whether it's Apple, Nike, or the Breadman, it's got to be something that people are passionate about because people want to be part of a community and share with other people. This kind of community building happened before the advent of social media, but of course social media has put it on steroids.

How do We Build Value into Our Product and Marketing?

- **Listen to the consumer**; go out and spend time in retail environments and gather marketing intelligence. We have spent many Saturdays in Target or at Macy's or Costco just browsing the aisles, listening to consumers talk about products. If the product they're discussing is yours or your competitors', listen and learn.

- **Go on the Internet** and read what consumers are saying about your product, and about competitive products.

- **Do not stuff the ballot box.** Don't go online and write fake reviews about your product—ever. You're going to get yourself in trouble, not only with your retail partners, but also with the Federal Trade Commission. False reviews sound fake; they don't ring true with customers, and that undercuts your product's credibility (as it should).

- **Don't forget the Golden Rule of Branding:** Treat other people exactly the way you want to be treated.

- **Under-promise, over-deliver.** Exceed your customer's expectations, preferably in unexpected and helpful ways. Give them more than they paid for; deliver unexpected value.

BARB

" One of my favorite examples of a winning combination of great industrial design with solid value is a homely little low-tech product—the Oxo Vegetable Peeler. Yes, it's just a vegetable peeler, but Oxo's Sam Farber reinvented it. Previously, vegetable peelers were all metal, so after peeling enough potatoes for a crowd, your hand would be sore. Then, inspired by his wife whose arthritis made it painful for her to peel potatoes, Farber developed a potato peeler with an ergonomic, rubberized handle. They created a product that was a joy to use because it peeled the potatoes well, and moreover, it was comfortable in your hand. So this wonderful new gadget checked many boxes:

- the senses, because it felt good in the hand and was comfortable to use

- satisfaction and joy, because the task no longer felt so cumbersome, and

- unexpected value, because its sturdy design meant it didn't fall apart after peeling a few batches of carrots or potatoes.

The crazy thing is that, as a consumer, I am no longer buying the usual $0.99 or $1.99 potato peeler. Instead, I'm happily spending $8.50 for the Oxo Vegetable Peeler. So, the retail price of the product went up on a multiple of four times for a functionality that was effectively the same. But what it delivers in terms of value, experience, and satisfaction is worth the multiple to me, and to many others who've happily embraced the Oxo brand. Now, you can find not only the Oxo peelers but dozens of other well-designed Oxo products hanging on pegboards at grocery stores, in large sections at Bed Bath & Beyond, and gourmet shops everywhere.

This is an important and relevant example of what happens when a trusted, desirable brand's team commits to excellence. It allows the company to legitimately command a higher price point and, in this case, to surround the brand with a dedicated community of loyal users. This is a simple product that built a foundation for a brand, which extends into many categories now, including baby care, gardening tools, and appliances. Oxo is a brand that appeals to consumers and which they'll gladly tell their best friends about. Again, the critical point here is listening to the consumer and creating products and services they ask for, delivered with trust, style, performance and quality. 🙸

Summary

Sam Farber made the consumer the hero—because his first consumer, his wife, was representative of a whole lot of other people in this aging boomer generation who are still doing most of the cooking. That little peeler created a community and a fan base of trust for his brand.

Change the way you look at product development and delivery. Instead of asking "How can I reduce costs?" ask "How can I deliver a higher value?"

CHAPTER SIX

Give Your Product Away

*"Your brand is a story unfolding across
all customer touch points."*

– Jonah Sachs, author, *Story Wars*

As much as the science of branding and its terminology have evolved
over the last twenty-five years, the basic foundational concepts haven't
changed that much. It's still a great idea to get your products into the
hands of who we used to call key opinion leaders (KOL), but who
are now known in our digital age as "influencers." What's the fastest,
most effective way to do that? Give your product away.

When the Sonicare electric toothbrush was introduced, we
made sure that many of the top dentists and periodontists in the
country received the products for free, because we knew their stamp
of approval would help influence thousands of people. Optiva, the
parent company of Sonicare, took a booth at the dental trade show at

the Moscone Center in San Francisco, and we gave Sonicare brushes to many high-level dentists and the heads of many dental schools, including those at Harvard Dental School and the University of Southern California Dental School. The goal was to have these KOLs try the product and then to have them positively influence the people with whom they came in contact about the product's great performance. We had the added benefit of recording their video testimonials as well to use throughout our D2C advertising campaigns.

We've both used celebrity and expert endorsements on almost every product in every category we've worked on. The difference is these kinds of endorsements came from people with a certain level of celebrity generated by traditional media outlets—those with followings through TV, radio, or print. Nowadays, they're more likely to be Internet personalities, thus, if you're selling a revolutionary baby bottle for instance, your best endorser might be an otherwise-unknown mommy blogger with a huge readership of potential customers.

BARB:

❝ Here's a priceless story that is a great example of unbridled opportunities: The George Foreman Grill benefitted tremendously from the celebrity endorsements, some of which were pure serendipity. The *New York Times* ran a story about the late Patrick Clark, the beloved chef at Tavern on the Green, who was hospitalized. When he couldn't stand the hospital food, he had someone smuggle a small-sized George Foreman Grill into his hospital room. Every day, someone from Tavern on the Green would drive uptown to deliver ingredients so that he could grill his own meals. A reporter from the

Times heard about it and did a story.[5] And in good faith, Salton helped underwrite a special chefs' dinner at the Tavern to celebrate Patrick Clark. You simply can't buy that kind of publicity, but occasionally it falls into your lap.

Another famous chef, Michael Chiarello, started using the grill too, and it quickly became the must-have appliance for many celebrated food personalities. A very prestigious French food company in New Jersey, D'Artagnan, used the grill during their food trade shows to prepare *foie gras*, because it's super-fast and it doesn't over cook the delicate goose liver. Many other famous foodies and influencers jumped on the bandwagon; they were preparing quail, fish, and vegetables on the grill at food shows as the product moved from being a cult favorite to mainstream. 🙿

Word of mouth and giving products away go hand in hand. But you've got to get the product to the right people, and in the right way.

- The influencer has to be "legitimate." What does that mean? Their expertise has to fit within the category of your product. Otherwise, their comments have little or no weight.

- Don't pay anybody for comments. They need to be authentic. Consumers either like your product or they don't like it. If they get paid, you have to disclose that they're being paid to endorse you, and the endorsement loses credibility.

---

5   Eric Asimov, "Patrick Clark, 42, is Dead; Innovator in American Cuisine," *New York Times*, February 13, 1998, https://www.nytimes.com/1998/02/13/nyregion/patrick-clark-42-is-dead-innovator-in-american-cuisine.html.

- You *must* follow disclosure guidelines. As of 2016, the FTC has put the bonus of disclosure on the manufacturer, not on the blogger or influencer. Wherever you are in the lifecycle of your campaign, you've got to pay attention to what that can mean for you because, as a manufacturer, *you* bear the responsibility.

And Here Are Some "Don'ts"

First, if you're producing a video or seeking an influencer to write glowing reports and that person happens to be a family member, you've got to disclose that. You can't stuff the ballot box. You have to tell the truth because being less than candid will inevitably come back to haunt you. We've worked with clients who have had family members show up to do on air testimonials who did not disclose to the agencies that this was a family member. But the Federal Trade Commission is clear on the requirement to meet full disclosure. In the digital arena, people are stretching or bending or breaking those rules almost on a daily basis. Don't be one of them.

Don't lie about your credentials. If you are a Nobel Laureate, that's great. But don't tell people that you have a Harvard or Yale degree when you actually just went there for a weekend symposium. Someone will research that, and there goes your credibility.

If you're hiring someone to endorse a beauty product but their taut skin owes more to a facelift or other procedure than to any effects the beauty product had on it, think about the consequences before you make that testimonial come to life. .

And again—don't use fake reviews because you're going to get your company and yourself in hot water. The largest retailers utilize behind-the-scenes protocols and tools within their programming which allow them to track the IP addresses of where those reviews are coming from. They can trace them back to their source. Perhaps you have your friends over for dinner, and you convince everyone to log onto their mobile devices (or your computer, for that matter) to write glowing, no-holds-barred reviews. After all, these are your friends, and how could anyone find out? Suddenly there's a cluster of ten reviews from the same IP locator address. Trust us, eventually this will get discovered, and the consequences are not on your objectives plan. Even Amazon has cracked down on the fake reviews. You'll see the notation "verified purchase" next to reviews on Amazon now. Be smart about your endorsements, and be creative.

RICK:

❝ A supplement company called Natural Stacks is a textbook example of how to use influencers the right way. Full disclosure: I'm on the board of advisors for the company.

Many of the supplements they sell are called nootropics or brain supplements, like dopamine and serotonin. They have a patented product called CILTEP that helps with memory and focus. When they first launched their products, they engaged with some high-level influencers like Tim Ferriss, the author of the *4-Hour Workweek*, a widely-read blogger and author with a huge online following. They also engaged with Dave Asprey, the creator of the Bulletproof Diet who also has a large online following of people that are interested in health. The third endorsement came from Martin Jacobson who won the World Series of Poker and was using their products to keep himself mentally sharp. The company provided their products to these folks to try for free, and they loved them and saw great results. Between these three people, they had the ability to influence literally millions of online followers. The result for the company was instant credibility for the brand and trust for the product line that turned into sales. They have been in business only a few years and have been growing at more than 100 percent per year. 🙾🙾

MEET YOUR AUDIENCE

Not all product giveaways go to celebrities, and you can build a great fan base if you're in the right place passing out your product to likely customers. Energy bars and drinks are popular giveaways at marathons, for instance.

Where's your demographic most likely to be located? If your product lends itself to sampling, be where your likely consumers are—with plenty of product and information on hand to meet your public. Get people to try your product; if they like it they will tell their friends and you are on your way. If there is something they don't like about it, that gives you valuable feedback to try and fix anything that will make your product better.

The Oprah Factor

When it comes to celebrity influencers, who's a more powerful personality than Oprah Winfrey? If Oprah says that a product is great, we all know what happens. Within minutes, the product's website crashes from the flood of people trying to buy, and stores sell out. Whether it's Spanx, a particular appliance, or a food product, it's suddenly everywhere, thanks to Oprah. Two products with which we were involved, Sonicare and Clarisonic, were both voted among Oprah's favorite products, and those endorsements had a huge effect on both businesses, creating more awareness for the brands and super-charging their sales up to the next level.

RICK:

❝ The Clarisonic cleansing brush is another good case study. When Barb was at Salton, they used to sell hundreds of thousands of rotational beauty brushes for a $19.99 price-point to retailers. These inexpensive brushes tended to be a Christmas gift item that was sold within housewares or personal care divisions. Then I was called on to help brand a new entry into the marketplace, a product called Clarisonic. It was a cleansing brush, too, but it wasn't priced at $19.99. Because of the underlying sonic technology, it was priced at $299. How do you get consumers to make that leap to a price point that's more than ten times the cost of a similar looking (though not similarly effective) product?

I'm not going to get into the technology, but there's something under the hood of this Clarisonic brush that does things those little rotational brushes don't do. I helped create some brand response advertising that explained its special properties, and the product tested out. We educated the consumer on the benefits that Clarisonic could provide that the cheaper brushes could not. Granted, in many ways, it was a leap of faith for the consumer to understand, "Why should I buy this brush when I can go to the drug store and buy something else to clean my face for under $20?" But the creators stood by their product. It's important to note too that the Clarisonic was sold in high-end department stores like Nordstrom, not in drug stores or housewares departments. It was positioned as the facial cleaning brush in the luxury market. And then, one day, Oprah told her studio audience that it was one of her favorite products to remove her makeup and the product took off. After several years they ended up selling the company to L'Oreal for $500 million.

This brings to mind a favorite quote of mine from Warren Buffet, who was a legendary investor: "Your premium brand had better be delivering something special, or it's not going to get the business." **"**

Keep Your Eyes on the Prize.

You never know where that influencer is going to come from that's going to move the needle, but you keep your eyes on the prize. It took three years of being on the market before Oprah endorsed Clarisonic.

Naturally, everyone who comes out of the gate says, "We need to get on ... " *Ellen*, or *Good Morning America*, or whatever the big talk show of the moment is. But that doesn't usually happen all at once; you have to start with baby steps, first getting your product in the hands of some smaller influencers that are easier to reach. This creates a groundswell that builds, and eventually, as you grow your following, you'll be able to reach those Oprah-level influencers. Pay for play is a big thing now, too: all of these "steals and deals" on the *Today Show, Good Morning America, Entertainment Tonight,* and *Access Hollywood* require a slotting fee to get a product into those giveaways. But to have a top influencer say, "I love this product," without getting a dime or a nickel for it is worth far more.

Using a good public relations firm can help jump start this process. Remember, this is part of the Omni-channel marketing mentioned in chapter 1 that you should always be looking to create. Following are some tips on how to do so.

The Importance of Supplementing Your Marketing with PR.

Your marketing campaign is designed to communicate, connect, and engage with your target audience. Making media publicity part of your marketing plan will:

- expedite getting your message out there because TV, magazines, newspapers, and radio definitely impact consumers. Did you know more people read magazines than ever, even if they are also on social media?

- optimize your credibility, because when people see a brand on a TV news segment, or on talk show, or in an article, the brand instantly gets the third-party endorsement from a trusted journalist;

- build you a respected reputation when the media coverage starts to snowball and influencers start getting in on the story.

Strategic media publicity placement is about getting your brand on mainstream TV shows, magazines, and newspapers that your target audience sees and trusts. This media exposure amps up all your DM activities because people are seeing and hearing about your brand more often and when they recognize your brand it creates positive familiarity that people trust. A third-party endorsement from media is another touch point and a very strong credential that your marketing campaign can benefit from.

Media publicity will create news that journalists want to report. It is the job of your PR liaison to come up with the story if it is not obvious to you. Don't fall for the trap that you only have news when you introduce a new product. Medical research, retail trends, fashions, celebrity activities, and seasonal interests are all what makes news, and your PR needs to be spotting and developing them. If you help journalists see and develop stories, they will report them and help you circulate your message to reach a larger number of people.

When you get media exposure you can often utilize it in your direct marketing (DM) spots. Either you can actually show the articles or TV segments or talk about them, as well as what celebrities, athletes, or ambassadors are saying about your brand as a result of your media publicity efforts, which gives your DM activities more credibility and believability.

> *A great marketing campaign, when amped by publicity, generates millions more impressions of all types.*

What this does over time is help build a brand, generate consumer demand, sell more product, and create a buzz that helps other people sell your brand to the people they know too. There's nothing as effective as making your customers proud that they know and use your brand. A great marketing campaign, when amped by publicity, generates millions more impressions of all types.

BARB:

" Accountability is, for me, the forefront of the relationship with PR agencies. It's my personal/professional practice to fully understand who is going to manage the account, take the initiative to drive impressions, and manage through both successes and crises. Kick the tires and make sure you know who is going to "drive the bus" on your account. **"**

The developers of GoPro cameras utilized the give–it-away strategy to kick-start their company two different ways. First, they sent out free cameras to the top surfers, snowboarders, skiers, mountain bikers, and other extreme athletes. It was the perfect marketing tool: these athletes would use the cameras to video tape their experiences as they surfed big waves or snowboarded down mountains, and they posted their videos online. Consumers would watch these cool videos and share them with their friends creating a viral marketing effect. Now every amateur athlete wanted a GoPro. The second way the free giveaway was used was in the TV advertising that we assisted in producing. These were classic brand response spots and all followed a similar format. Each thirty-second spot started with a brand logo, and then there was a short clip of user-generated footage which GoPro got for free from the extreme athletes. At the end of each spot we included a giveaway: "Win one of everything GoPro makes, every day." That contest drove consumers to the GoPro site (www.gopro.com) to register their email address to try and win the daily prize. Once on the site, they'd see other cool videos they could share with their friends. While they were there, they might purchase a GoPro camera, helping to offset the advertising costs. Thus, GoPro then had a database of names of their target customers to whom they could re-market—simple, but brilliant. That's how GoPro went from a start-up to a billion-dollar company in about eight years—by giving away their products to the right people.

Loyalty, Word of Mouth, and Brand Ambassadors

When it comes to loyalty programs and brand ambassadors, the key to success is building community. Where do your potential community members they live? They live on social media.

Apple doesn't have to pay its fans to rave about their products; the fans set up their own websites to do it for them. Aspire toward this type of loyalty as your own brand goal.

It's important to remember, however, that your social media strategy can't be all about selling. It's not about getting that credit card, and it's not pushing your consumer to "buy today" at every turn. It's about building community, trust, frequency, and loyalty. You do that with user-generated content; you do it with content that speaks to the hearts and souls of your followers. Content marketing is one of the best ways to build a loyal customer following.

If yours is a beauty product, for instance, that can mean sharing skin tips or results photos and getting people to post their selfies. It's always surprising how much people will share if they feel as though they're part of a community.

BARB:

As the chief marketing officer of HoMedics, we participated in a series of national events, one of which was Oprah's *Live Your Best Life Tour*. Her weight was a much-discussed and covered story, which clearly resonated with her fans. Her audience related to the challenges of being on a diet, the ups and downs and feelings of shame or success. Oprah was the featured speaker, so the exhibition hall was packed with thousands of her loyalists. We were there to exhibit the high-end scales made by HoMedics that also measured body fat and water; we offered a complimentary weigh-in at the HoMedics booth with four weigh stations. In no time there were lines of hundreds of women waiting to be weighed and to learn about their body fat and water. Given how sensitive most women are about their weight, this was a tremendous endorsement of Oprah's power with that audience. 🙦

As a Founder, You Can Be a Powerful Ambassador.

When you're starting out, those celebrity endorsements are tough to come by. But as a founder you've got a lot going for you: enthusiasm and product knowledge. You know what you're selling and you know what it does. In the early days of Dyson when they were a fledgling company, James Dyson was the spokesman on their television commercials. He basically just said the same four words over and over: "It doesn't lose suction." That became the product tagline. Floor care is a dog-eat-dog business, but pretty soon everyone was talking about this oddball vacuum cleaner because the message was simple, memorable, and to the point—"It doesn't lose suction."

We see lots of stories, especially in natural foods, about how a founder or product person was inspired by some amazing find—a new berry or grain or whatever—to create a product. As long as the story is authentic and resonates with people's hearts and minds, it makes a big difference.

GoPro's founder story was a great one, too. The founder, Nick Woodman, was coming off of a failed Internet business when he took a year off to travel around the world with his girlfriend. One day while he was surfing in Australia, he watched while the pro-surfers were getting great photos of themselves by using professional photographers. He wanted some photos of himself surfing, but he was frustrated because he couldn't afford to hire a professional photographer. So, he bought a cheap waterproof camera, found a way to attach it to his wrist, and was able to take pictures of himself without hiring a professional photographer. Other surfers started asking him about it, and he realized he was onto something. He started selling these homemade cameras in surf stores up and down the West Coast, and thus a business was born. He was his own first and best customer, and that gave him the credibility on which to build the community of GoPro sports enthusiasts.

Mrs. Fields started her cookie empire by passing out free samples. So did Wally Amos of Famous Amos. Those stories and those founders became part of the mythology of the brands—and samples turned into sales. It is a simple way of building your brand that has worked for many different products in many different categories. We consider this one of our favorite timeless marketing tips.

Getting your product to the right people for endorsements isn't rocket science—but you do need to get creative. Today's Internet-driven consumer culture offers all kinds of opportunities to connect with your potential community and to reach those influencers who can make your product a household name.

SUMMARY

Don't underestimate the power of giving away product. It doesn't matter if you're a startup or if you have no money, giving your product away to the right people is the ultimate guerilla, grassroots marketing. It lets you put your product in the hands of people who can influence large followings, and it's a very simple, inexpensive way to start the brand building process.

CHAPTER SEVEN

Always Listen to Your Customers

"Mass advertising can help build brands, but authenticity is what makes them last. If people believe they share values with a company, they will stay loyal to the brand."

—Howard Schultz, former CEO of Starbucks

As you introduce your product and your brand to the world, your best source of feedback isn't going to be paid focus groups or random surveys; it's going to be your customers. Brand building key number four: always listen to your customers. They'll tell you what they think in a remarkably unfiltered way, and what they tell you is worth more than any paid research you can get.

Remember the story of the George Foreman Grill: At its introduction, its inventor saw it as a home fajita maker, and it was that original version—the Fajita Express—that Barb and other Salton execs introduced at the annual Gourmet Show in San Francisco.

When the product was called the Fajita Express, retailers didn't bite. Their responses ran to, "The food smells funny," and "Who needs this?" It was just an item with a function. It *wasn't* an item with a story—and story matters. It's critical when you're creating a brand or an item that you create a story around it that's compelling. The product was a failure initially because it didn't have a heart and soul; it did not have personality and it didn't have a story. Just like a person, a brand needs a unique personality. When it was rebranded and given a compelling story, the same product—the exact same product—enjoyed tremendous success.

What Sets You Apart from Your Competition?

With every product we work on, we always ask the visionaries—the founders, the creators, and inventors—the same questions: What is your dream for this product? Where do you see it going? What differentiates your product from everything else that's out there in the market? What are the touch points that will make this product desirable to the consumer? That leads us down to research into the brand and the product lines—getting this from a third-party with an objective point of view is key. Then we do a SWOT analysis. As an example, let's say you've invented what you're certain is the best hand-held can opener the world has ever seen—but will it be a viable product in the marketplace? That's where your SWOT analysis comes into play.

First, we ask, "What are the strengths of your product?" Perhaps it's especially easy to use, and ergonomic in its design. What are the weaknesses? Maybe it doesn't work on cat-food cans. What are your opportunities? Research shows there's a new kind of can coming onto the market, and your opener is the only one that can open it. What are the threats? The threats come into play in a couple of different ways, such as competitively. Maybe there's a large consumer product company out there that has made a can opener that looks and feels like your idea, and because they have a huge manufacturing and marketing force behind them, they can bring it to market faster, quicker, cheaper. Or maybe the threat is coming from the food industry, which is packaging shelf-stable foods in pouches or other packaging that doesn't require an opener. You need to know the size of your market to understand your product's potential: is there an international market for it?

But in that initial product testing stage, we find that we always get the best, most honest, and most useful feedback from real customers using the product.

Keep in Touch with Your Customers, and Follow Up on Their Experiences.

We have always had the most success working with companies that have already had a product out in the marketplace and that has had some paying customers, regardless of the level of sales. It is the concept of market place validation. People are already paying for the product, they like it, so then it becomes a simple case of creating more awareness for the product. This is done with the omni-channel D2C Marketing that we talk about in chapter 9.

One of the first steps we take is to interview twenty to thirty existing customers. We do this for every product we work on, and did this for every one of the products we've mentioned in the book. We ask standardized questions to measure their interactions with the product: How did you hear about our product? Where did you purchase it? Why did you buy this product? What do you like or dislike about it? How do you use it in your home? Would you recommend this product to other people? Why or why not? If you were talking to a friend about this product, what would you tell them? These questions vary for every product. We keep these sessions as conversational in tone as we can, and often the next question is based on the person's response, so the interviews take on a free-flowing form. Never try to force people to say what you want to hear.

After we've looked at the videos and read through transcripts of the responses, we begin to see trends taking shape in the answers we're getting—especially around what people like, what they might dislike, and questions or concerns they might have that need to be addressed in our marketing.

When we take the next step to creating the brand response advertising, all the information we need to build a successful marketing campaign is there in these responses. We always video the people we're talking to and make transcripts of the answers as we're doing our product research so that we can feature the best excerpts or "sound bites" from those interviews as authentic product testimonials.

If we're working with a product that's already in the market, we reach out directly to people in the customer database and ask them if they're happy with the product and whether they'd be willing to be interviewed. Some people don't want to talk about it on camera, but others do, so we might start with a list of fifty people and end up finding twenty that are delighted to speak with us. Out of those twenty, we usually end up with six to eight really good testimonials.

But what if it's a brand-new product that hasn't yet been introduced in the marketplace? Many people will use a focus group in this situation, but we try to avoid those whenever possible because, in our experience, the information obtained is not as useful. Instead we pass the new product out to at least twenty people that we feel are in the right demographic and ask them to use it for thirty days. This takes a little work, but the results are worth it. Then we go back to our new customers with our list of questions and get the feedback and information we need to help us in our marketing. It is always a good idea to video these people to create some real testimonials for the product, and it creates valuable content that can be used in other social media channels.

When we're launching a new product, we incentivize people by letting them keep the product for participating in the trial. But we never pay people to get responses; they're very authentic, real-user responses. This differs from standard focus groups in that generally people aren't nearly as familiar with the product as they need to be to provide valuable feedback. Also, in a focus group setting, people's answers are usually influenced by other people's answers, and that changes the dialogue. When we do our individual interviews, however, the person talking to us doesn't know what the person before said or what the person following them will say, so it's more genuine.

Real Time Feedback

QVC provides a unique window into customer and purchasing behavior because you know in real time when a host or guest says something on TV that sparks a sudden spike in call volume. George Foreman would go on the show to promote his grill; he and the host would demonstrate how it worked, and every time George took a bite of food, the call volumes would spike. People just loved watching him eat! His responses were very natural and unscripted, and viewers responded to his authenticity by phoning in and buying the product. Naturally we capitalized on that, and in our subsequent advertising we always made sure to show him eating a lot—and the shows performed better and better.

Get Social

Social media provides us with a new way to listen to customer feedback. Social media can be like a brush fire: when it's negative, it can be hard to put out. Word of mouth is more personal; in direct marketing, we used to call it TAF, or tell a friend. But with the advent of mommy bloggers in the last ten years, product reviews are shared instantly with their virtual friends. These moms are testing products; if they don't like it then they return it to Costco, but if they love it then they'll share photos and rave about it with their friends—and word travels fast. Like it or not, we've become a society of critics.

For an example of the power of the consumer review, look at travel: who could have predicted that AirBnb would have travelers staying in private homes, which they'd then review? Suddenly that consumer is empowered to become an authority. I can give Jim or Jeanie—whoever is offering up their room for rent—a four-star review or five-star review if I enjoyed my time there—or I can give them no stars and slam their accommodations or service and other potential customers will take note. This is a robust and powerful equation between the consumer and the product. The review itself has evolved to be a very powerful platform. Everyone is going to get a less-than-ideal review occasionally—because there are some people who simply can't be pleased—but generally the reviewer is going to be seen by consumers as an unbiased authority.

How to Be Social Savvy

Use your social media platform to get your message out to position your brand as an authority and resource, to stay in sight and in mind, and to facilitate a two-way conversation with your audience. By using a combination of social media channels that are relevant to your audience, you can communicate your message more effectively and efficiently—where they are, when they are there, and in the form that they are searching for information.

Cater to your audience. Be a fly on the wall and use the intel that is readily available to you. Share information that is useful and relevant by paying attention to what people are saying about your brand and your industry. Remember, social media channels are simply a window into an ongoing conversation and you are being given a "pass" to listen in (and participate where appropriate). So, be sure you aren't just talking to yourself—listen first, then participate if you are able to add value; don't just walk into the room and start talking.

K.I.S.S.—keep it simple, stupid. Don't overthink it, don't over-complicate it. Make friends. Play nice. Find ways to make people want to become your fan: share interesting and relevant content that matters to your audience, be real, be sincere, have fun, show your company's personality, and be true to your message—phoniness comes across loud and clear, even when you are not physically standing right in front of someone. Remember,

Remember, social media channels are simply a window into an ongoing conversation and you are being given a "pass" to listen in (and participate where appropriate). So, be sure you aren't just talking to yourself— listen first, then participate if you are able to add value; don't just walk into the room and start talking.

above anything else, build relationships. Be consistent, present, and genuine in all of your communication. People appreciate "real." People do business with people they know, like, and trust. Refer to the principles set forth in Dale Carnegie's *How to Win Friends and Influence People* and apply them to your business.

Slow and steady wins the race; never buy fans. Sure, you can have everyone at your "party" by offering *x, y,* and *z,* but will any of them help you clean up in the morning? Getting a thousand Twitter followers in a week, or five thousand Facebook fans in a month, or twenty thousand newsletter subscribers, or a hundred thousand website visitors, or even one million hits on a video on your YouTube channel does not happen overnight, and takes a concerted, consistent, and persistent effort. It's just like making friends—the bond could be sealed in one night, but a true friendship, just like any relationship, takes a long time to build.

Be methodical with regard to sharing content. Develop and use an editorial calendar to help you organize your content posting strategy. Think about using a content theme for each month and develop your ideas around that theme. Doing this will help you avoid an "all-over-the-board" appearance and ensure that you don't repeat yourself and that you cover all the important points that are relevant to your message and goals—and most importantly, that you are answering your audience's questions to move them down the sales path. Lay it out for at least three months at a time (ideally for the year) and incorporate major holidays and yearly (or one-time) events that impact your industry. Bottom line, the more planned out your strategy is, the more clearly you will be able to communicate your message and in the most timely manner. Don't be bashful about riding "the content wave" when there is something happening in the media that everyone is talking about; use that story and find a way to tie it into your message and make it relevant to what you are doing.

New content can come in the form of an opinion piece about something happening in your industry, a review of an industry-related article, offering a tip or advice, or even getting a testimonial from one of your clients—the list goes on and on. Bottom line—post new and fresh content at least two to three times per week to keep both the search engines and users interested. Use Google Alerts to get news you can use. Set up an alert for each of your keywords and for the names of entities that are important to your industry (use quotations around proper names to make sure you get targeted results). Get inspired for your own writing for your blog.

Follow the 80/10/10 rule when sharing on social media channels: talk about your industry or related news 80 percent of the time, share your brand's news or promos 10 percent of the time, relate the news to what your company offers the other 10 percent. This helps to solidify you as a resource and authority and helps you garner more followers so that when you do have something to "sell" they will be more likely to listen.

If you're not including video in your efforts, you're missing the boat. You can pre-record your videos or live-stream from Facebook or YouTube. Keep in mind it does not have to be perfect as long as there is valuable information contained in it. Don't spend a lot of money on video production—people do not visit YouTube or any other video sharing site and expect to find professional quality video. Use the video camera on your smart phone to film short video clips whenever you are out and about at conferences, events, client meetings; give folks a "behind the scenes" look into a "day in the life" at your organization. Make relevant and interesting videos that are short and to the point. Not sure what to film? Ask your audience what they want to see. Take your FAQs and answer them in a video, show people how to do something, demonstrate a product, and on and on. Take a look at what your competition is doing and what is getting a lot of views—then take those ideas, put your own spin on it, get creative, and have fun with it. What would you want to see? Ideally, your videos should be sixty seconds or less to gain and hold the users' interest.

Don't Even Think about Faking It.

We've talked in a couple of chapters about the dangers of posting fake reviews, but it bears repeating. Whether you yourself write them, ask friends and relatives to do so, or even hire someone to provide them for you: don't do it. Don't risk squandering whatever credibility you have on the chance of being unmasked. Someone will notice, and someone will call you out on it—publically. The last thing any new brand or company needs is an FTC or legal meeting regarding clustered, falsified, or paid for reviews. Nearly as bad is the tendency to get nasty or confrontational in their responses to bad reviews. If you feel you must respond, begin with "I'm sorry that your experience with our product wasn't everything you hoped for," and continue in that tone. Resist the temptation to question their taste, their intelligence, or their motives. Apologize, and take steps to make the situation better.

Will Your Customers Know How to Use What You're Selling Them?

Have you ever brought home a new electronic gadget only to discover that you can't make the darned thing work? It's a frustrating experience that leaves you asking, "Is this thing broken, or am I just not smart enough to operate it?"

One way to keep this from happening (and to keep those disgruntled customers from slamming you in reviews) is to do your due diligence before you release the product. Are the directions clear enough that the average person can understand them (assuming he or she actually reads them, which is not necessarily going to happen)? How can you make its operation more intuitive? Apple's done a brilliant job of making its powerful little computer disguised as a phone easy for most people to use, and they're rewarded with tremendous loyalty for that. That didn't happen by accident. Do your own usability and anthropological studies, because there's no other way to see past your own understanding of the product to how someone without your investment will interact with it. Get your subjects to sign a non-disclosure agreement—then let them kick the tires.

If customers contact you to register their disappointment, outrage, or confusion, make sure they're treated respectfully and that the exchange ends when your customer service department has made the situation right—whatever that takes. Replacing or refunding may cost you, but you'll reap the benefits in positive word of mouth, both in person and in product reviews on the Internet. It's like the way neighbors in the old days talked over the fence: "Have you heard how great this company is? I used their product, and when it broke down, they replaced it for me immediately."

Talking Heads versus Reality Testimonials

As tastes change and evolve, how we frame our marketing has to change too, and that's especially true with the video or TV advertising that we do. In the old days, we used to sit our filming subjects on chairs, typically in a living room or a kitchen, and we'd interview them. That's what called a "talking head," but that simple technique just isn't as effective as it used to be. With all of the reality shows on TV and people making their own videos, that type of advertising doesn't work as well as what we call "reality testimonials." These might be something you shoot live at a tradeshow, for instance, with the people who come up to your booth. This kind of footage feels more real and unrehearsed, and today's consumer responds to that feeling of immediacy and authenticity.

Here are some tips on live interviewing techniques that work for us:

- Get your subject talking first; don't ask whether they like or dislike your product—just ask how they feel about it.

- Be ready for a classic "deer in headlights" response, which is most people's initial reaction to being filmed. They're liable to shut down to simply answering "yes" or "no" if you give them the opportunity, so don't; ask questions that require them to speak at more length.

- When you get someone who wants to talk, don't interrupt with more questions; just let them talk. Nod, be responsive, take notes to show you're listening, but let them talk. You can go back and ask more specific questions based on what they've said. For instance, when we were interviewing people about the George Foreman Grill, someone could say, "I like the fact that it's very convenient. I can just come home from work, grab something out of the refrigerator, throw it on there, and two minutes later it's ready." As the interviewer, you could follow up with, "So, what you like about it is the fact that it's convenient. It saves you time," and see how they respond.

- Focus on that benefit; use what that consumer has said as a prompt for your next interviews: "Tell me about how convenient this product is to use at home. How does it help you when you come home from work? How does it help you prepare meals for your family?" Hone in on that one particular benefit of the product. Another consumer might say, "I can't believe how great the food tastes when it comes off the grill." That gives us the prompt for the next interview: "Why do you like the taste? What's different about the flavor the food has, cooking it this way versus the way you normally cook food?"

- Be alert to any negative answer trends coming out of the interviews: If we're interviewing thirty consumers and all thirty say, "I don't like the fact it takes too long to heat up," or something like that, then that's information that should go back to the manufacturer: "You've got to do something about this. People are waiting ten minutes for your grill to heat up and it's going to be an issue." That feedback can provide vital help in fine-tuning the product and making it better. You're not going to have a successful brand if there are issues out there that people are concerned about.

Build a Customer Database

Your share of loyal customers creates profits and long-term value for your business. You've got to keep the big picture in view; you don't want to settle for a one-time sale because then you have to work too hard and spend too much to keep repeating that sale over and over again. Building a customer database is one of the most important keys to success in growing both your business and your brand. You can use this database to get customer feedback that can offer you priceless insights to what they'd like to buy from you in the future—

When you're building your business, you want as many loyal customers as you can get so that you can remarket to them. If they like your first product, then there's a good chance they'll like your second product.

if they're telling you what they want in a product or future products. When you're building your business, you want as many loyal customers as you can get so that you can remarket to them. If they like your first product, then there's a good chance they'll like your second product.

Here's a good example: When we were marketing the Juiceman juice extractor we developed a relationship with our customers by constantly providing them with the latest nutritional information. This is what's called content marketing. Our factory in China came up with an upgrade to the exiting cutting blade in the juicer that would provide up to 20 percent more juice from the same amount of produce. We sent a postcard (this was pre-internet; now, you would use email) with this information to our customer database. That one simple postcard generated over $500,000 in sales!

Listening to the feedback that your customers give you can help you to deliver either a more desirable new product to them or improve an existing product. Just remember, it's much easier to sell something to someone that bought something from you once than it is to get a new customer every time.

Don't Shoot the Messenger.

We've talked about the negative impact that founder's syndrome can have in marketing, and that's very true in this area. Nobody hates hearing negative things about a product more than its inventor. It's as though the critical feedback they get from a customer is aimed straight at them and not their product, and that can cause them to dismiss it. Be honest with yourself: if you're not capable of listening to critical feedback and keeping an open mind about it, then hire someone to do it for you, because your customers are telling you the hard truth, delivering real and valuable information to you that you can't afford to dismiss. We have been in situations where a founder or inventor will tie himself in knots trying to justify why he shouldn't pay attention to what consumers are trying to tell him—it's the wrong group, or the product is just being positioned incorrectly, etc., etc. This benefits nobody, and it can really come back to bite you. Get your ego out of the way.

Again, remember the story of the *Emperor's New Clothes*? We recently worked with a client who's too much like that emperor for his own good. The challenge is compounded by the fact that the people around him are too intimidated (or worried about their jobs) to tell him the truth about what they heard again and again from consumers regarding problems with his product. Nobody wants to say, "You're naked." Everybody's scared to tell the truth. Nobody wants to be the bad guy. But sooner or later, the truth will prevail. You wouldn't believe how many potentially successful products get derailed because people in a business are afraid to deliver honest insights because they don't want to challenge the perception of the person above them, or of the person leading the company. We've seen it happen more times than we can count, and that's a recipe for failure. You've got to keep an open mind and open heart and be willing to listen. Founders will say, "Yeah, I want negative feedback" then reject it when it's given, but the market is always going to tell you what it wants. Founders try to force feed their ideas into that system, and they run up against the wall of people saying, "No, that's not what we want."

If you find yourself resisting or trying to rationalize negative feedback, check out the title of this chapter—and remember, always listen to your customer!

Summary

Your customers are the best source of honest feedback about your product or service. This information can be used to build your marketing message, and to improve your product in its next iteration. Just like a person, a brand needs a personality. What is the personality of your brand?

:

CHAPTER EIGHT

World-Class Customer Service

*"Making promises and keeping them is
a great way to build a brand."*

—Seth Godin, author, *The Dip*

The most effective branding starts after the sale. In an ever-more crowded, border-free marketplace, great customer service and aftermarket care remain absolutely essential to building a trusted brand. That's true regardless of the distribution channel you're selling in, whether it's online, on Amazon, in brick-and-mortar stores, or all of the above.

It's been said that "customer service is not a department; it's an attitude" and we believe in that wholeheartedly. Every great brand we

> *In an ever-more crowded, border-free marketplace, great customer service and aftermarket care remain absolutely essential to building a trusted brand.*

built has delivered exceptional customer service, which enables us to create a long-term relationship with our customers, helps to foster brand loyalty, and also allows us to introduce new products when the time is right. That's the power of having a good relationship with your customer. If you over-deliver on customer service just like you do with your product, your customers will continue to put their trust in you over time—even with new products and new services. So if you are arbitrating goods on Amazon and eBay, how will you handle FTC compliance, returns, claims and defectives? Who is answering your 800-number? Or online chatbot?

Why is Customer Service So Critical?

The typical customer experience goes something like this: Your customer buys your product and gets it home. There's roughly a 5 percent chance the customer will actually read the instruction manual. That means that if there's a problem, they are going to call your 800-number or email you, because it's just easier to do. If they are Internet-savvy, they may go onto the web to look for help and find a YouTube video showing them how to use it, but a good percentage of your customers won't do that. They'll simply call you to ask questions, complain, and to be walked through whatever they don't understand. The bottom line is they need help, and how well you help them will define their feelings about your company and your brand every bit as much as the initial advertising and the product itself.

With online marketing becoming more prevalent, people are increasingly removed from direct conversation with other people in making their transactions. Companies seem to be moving toward even more automation, striving to have as few customer touches as possible in transactions. But what separates highly successful

Internet businesses from their competition is that their brands are built as much or more on great customer service as they are on the products themselves. A company like Zappos is a great example that has emerged from this world and created a phenomenal brand. The benefit to building that brand? Being purchased by Amazon for over $800 million! Great customer service doesn't go out of style; it's always been one of the foundational pillars of building a great brand, and you'll never get there unless you live, breathe, and offer it daily.

What Does That Mean in Practice?

It really goes back to this crazy, old-fashioned notion of service with a smile and "the customer is always right." Sam Walton said it best: "There is only one boss: the customer. And he can fire everybody in the company from the chairman on down, simply by spending his money somewhere else."

Nordstrom's is famous for their world-class customer service. They started as a shoe store in Seattle, expanding to a high-end department store best known for fashion brands. But truly, their entire business reputation was built on one simple premise, a "no questions asked" customer service policy. You could buy a pair of shoes there, wear them for three years, then take them back and be given a new pair if you had a complaint, "no questions asked." Most people would think, "Won't people take advantage of that, creating a huge expense?" And yes, inevitably there will be a certain number of people that will take advantage of a liberal customer service policy. But it also shows that you stand behind your product and your brand, and that's the one differentiator that built the entire Nordstrom chain from a little shoe store in Seattle to a retailing giant. Customers trust them, and are willing to pay higher prices than they might find elsewhere for the comfort of having that kind of guarantee. It breaks down the barriers to purchase.

RICK:

❝ When we were building the Juiceman brand, many companies were farming out their customer service departments to third-party providers, preferring to leave customer service problems to them. But we did everything internally; at one point we had one hundred and eighty employees and the customer service department was the largest department in the company. Our philosophy was that we would do anything to help people with any type of problem, and customers responded by trusting us and spreading great word of mouth. There's no substitute for satisfied customers who tell their friends, "You can trust this company. They'll bend over backward to help you. If you have a problem with your product, they'll fix it." It creates an atmosphere of trust.

Make Lemonade ... and Profits

The most interesting revelation we had was that our customer service department actually turned into a profit center. How? Usually, if you help people solve a problem, they're happy with you and they trust you, so they become more open to buying more of your products. When a customer called in with an issue about the product, we would first solve the person's problem. Then, since we had other products, we would just ask them at the end of the conversation, "Would you be interested in learning more about this other product?" More often than not they would say yes, and we turned an initial negative experience into a positive customer sale. Clearly customer service, if done correctly, doesn't have to be an expense—and can even become a profit center.

Good customer service isn't something you can afford to shrug off, because in today's social media-driven marketplace, people will hear that you don't stand behind your product. There's no quicker way to shoot yourself in the foot.

Now, nobody enjoys getting customer complaints—and it's natural to even feel a degree of resentment if the product is your baby. But how you look at complaints is something you can change. Start by seeing this negative feedback as lemons waiting to be made into lemonade. Think of customer complaints as a real-time focus group. That's a better attitude than, "Oy, here's another one." The customer service team needs to have regular meetings with the marketing, product management, and product development teams. Talk to each other so you can improve your product. Don't rest on your laurels. You're getting direct feedback from the customer, and if it just stops in the customer service department, what good is it? When you connect the team receiving that feedback to the marketing department and the product development department, that feedback turns into useful information.

When we started the Juiceman business, the juicer we were buying had a lot of mechanical problems and constantly broke down. While our customers loved the juice, they didn't like the mechanical issues. We decided to manufacture our own juicer with a design based on customer feedback. The first juicer had a small feeder tube, and our customers complained that larger vegetables like big carrots would get stuck in it, so we increased the size of the feeder tube. We were also hearing that the motor bogged down when customers were processing a lot of vegetables at once, so we added a larger and more powerful motor. Addressing those complaints helped us to build a better product and that lead to increased sales.

Amazon has taken this "use the feedback to improve the product" idea to new heights with the Echo device. The interface, Alexa, takes voice commands via the Echo and follows them. Amazon follows up on the efficacy of Alexa's execution by listing out all the commands you gave on your dashboard, and asking whether or not Alexa properly followed your instructions.

That feedback goes to the product developers working on voice control, so they can continue to refine and improve the interface between you and that product. Apple's Siri, on the other hand, offers no opportunity to do much more than yell at your phone when Siri fails to hear and/or respond properly to your commands (in our experience, too much of the time).

Another "lemons into lemonade" story happened with Sonicare. The company struggled with an issue early on in their selling cycle, when a handful of customers complained that the handle of the toothbrush got hot. Even though it was only a few complaints out of thousands of units they'd sold, Sonicare decided to take a proactive approach, and instead of waiting to see if this would snowball, they recalled all of the units that were out in the marketplace and replaced every single one of them. That choice cost the company millions of dollars—but bought them tremendous credibility via positive press and PR that helped take the company to the next level. By getting out in front of customer issues and going above and beyond what necessarily would be required of good service, they boosted their brand past what any ad campaign could have accomplished. 🙶

Consumers Do the Darndest Things.

If you offer a "no questions asked" replacement guarantee, you'd better honor it. We actually had a customer send back a juicer with a letter explaining that he'd somehow put a twenty-two-caliber bullet down the feeder chute of the juicer. The bullet went off into the motor. The motor conked out. We called him up and talked to him about it—and we ended up replacing the juicer, with a strict warning to "stop juicing bullets!" Even though the malfunction clearly wasn't our fault, we followed through. Some people would look at this as a needless expense, a better way of looking at it is that you are creating valuable brand equity.

BARB

66 Once my company had to deal with a furious customer who returned a coffee maker with a borderline-abusive letter explaining that he'd poured a can of tomato soup in it, along with a can full of water, and the darned thing wouldn't make soup in his coffee carafe. They explained to him that coffee makers aren't really equipped to handle viscous liquids, but they took it back and gave him a refund. Crazy? Yes, on one level—but you've also got to think of it in terms of, "I can resolve this customer service complaint for less than $30." Plus, we ended up with a happy customer.

Another customer contacted us via a furious letter, saying that he'd been annoyed at the slow speed of his home bread machine's baking process, so he'd taken the metal loaf pan out of the machine and put it in his microwave. He was furious when the bread pan exploded in a rain of sparks and was demanding a new microwave! That was one time we said no, but we did accept the return of his bread machine. 99

Some marketers are great at marketing and generating initial sales, but fall short when it comes to follow up customer service. Good marketers can make money by getting a lot of people to buy their products over the short term, but without the long-term customer service component, they'll never succeed in building a great brand.

Create a Community of Brand Ambassadors.

As we've noted, most of what you hear via customer service will likely be complaints—but social media gives you the opportunity to build a robust community of customers online where you can interact with your brand advocates in a positive way. A lot of that is going to come from what we call "user-generated content"—blogs, typically. For an idea of what's possible, look at the direct-to-consumer company Beach Body, which markets fitness training programs. They are phenomenal at building community and getting customers to post before and after shots of themselves in their bathing suits or workout clothes. These are posted on their sites and used in advertising—and the company sends the customer a branded t-shirt as a thank you. Wearing that shirt tells people, "I'm in a special club."

Victoria's Secret is best known for its fashion show, but their real customer base is the young women who buy PINK, an internal house brand. They wear PINK brand jogging suits that have "PINK" written across the bottom or down the leg. Again, there's that sense of belonging to a cool community.

We talked in an earlier chapter about delivering value, and one of the most powerful ways to do this is to surprise and delight your customer by under-promising and over-delivering. Obviously, a customer who gets less than he was promised is not going to become a brand ambassador, but if they get not only a great product but some little extras in the box, they'll tell their friends.

Dealing with Unhappy Customers: Do's and Don'ts

- DO everything you can to resolve a customer's complaint, even if it costs you money. Yes, there's always going to be that one crank out there who simply cannot be pleased, no matter what you do, and whose joy in life is making complaints. But more often than not, in doing so you will have created a satisfied customer who will be glad to buy from you again.

- DON'T let your sense of pique move you to respond in a snippy or undignified way to a customer complaint or review. The public will invariably side with the customer if you show anything less than care and courtesy.

- DO take the time to give a thoughtful answer—which can be as simple as "We're very sorry that you had this experience. Thank you for letting us know about this problem. Our goal is to deliver a great product and great service to our customers every time." Make sure you mention your customer care department, and either ask them to get in touch, or arrange to have their complaint followed up on.

- DO make sure that the people in your customer care department share your commitment to customer service and that they're trained (and better yet, scripted) to handle whatever comes their way with grace and good cheer. Don't leave them unskilled or underprepared to deal with angry or unhappy customers, because from the customer's point of view they *are* your company. It's amazing how far a heartfelt "I'm sorry" can go to salve irritated feelings.

- DO follow up on every customer complaint resolution via an email or notecard sent to the customer at their address along the lines of, "We're so glad that you're happy and that we could repair this. Here's our website; please like us on Facebook," etc. Close the loop with a smile and a handshake, and pass on a great feeling about your brand to that customer.

Sometimes it Pays to Pause and Reboot.

If you're overwhelmed by bad reviews, you've got to act decisively if you're going to save your brand. It doesn't matter if you're a one-person operation handling all aspects of your enterprise or a very large company; if you're starting to get a lot of bad reviews, hit the brakes on your marketing so you're not pumping more product into the system and creating more bad reviews. Slow that down until you solve the problems with the product, and then start your marketing again. Remember, the snowball effect can work both positively and negatively, and social media just helps the snowball get bigger, faster. If you ignore repeated complaints and stubbornly persist in marketing a not-great product, you're just splashing a little bit more gas on the fire.

What's the worst possible response to a consumer complaint? Ignoring it. If somebody is reaching out for help or has a problem and nobody gets in contact with them or they can't get through to you, you're just creating more frustration.

Never forget the Golden Rule of Branding. It's very simple, and it's based on the philosophy embodied in the "Golden Rule": treat your customers exactly the same as you would want to be treated.

Think back to the last time you bought some product or service, and put yourself in their shoes.

When interacting with a customer, remember:

- Consumers have no desire to be put on hold for ten minutes to wait for an answer.

- Buyers expect prompt delivery of a product, especially when it was promised *fast*.

- Customers frown upon rude or haughty treatment.

- When deciding how to deal with customers, always begin by thinking in terms of what response would make *you* happy if you were in their shoes. Frame your response accordingly, with all the helpfulness and courtesy you can muster. When you do this consistently, it can add real power and strength to your brand.

Customer Service Action Exercise

Anonymously call up (or email) your own office/store/support team and ask a pointed question about your product or service, and then give a grade based on how well you honestly think your system worked to treat you the way you wanted to be treated. Be brutally honest. This isn't meant to be used as a "gotcha!" on your team members. You own the system and the processes used; it's your business, so *you* own this grade as well.

Summary

The most effective branding starts after the sale! Don't minimize the importance of this.

CHAPTER NINE

Timeless Marketing Secrets

"Good marketing makes the company look smart.
Great marketing makes the customer feel smart."

– Joe Chernov, former head of content for HubSpot

Many things change in the marketing world—advertising tactics and style, delivery methods, distribution channels, demographics, etc.—but certain marketing concepts never grow old because they've always worked to increase sales and profits and they always will. Understanding and applying these timeless marketing truths to your marketing efforts will help you realize a maximum return on your investment, create greater brand awareness, and spur company growth. The following ten tips are what we have found time and time again to be effective.

Timeless Marketing Tip 1: Always Upsell

There is *always* something else you can sell. Once a customer has bought your product and is satisfied, you need to offer them complementary products that piggy-back on the original sale. If you sell moisturizer, you should also be offering skin cleanser. If you're selling an espresso maker, you should be selling a milk foamer or a subscription coffee service to go with it. This is the 80-20 rule; 80 percent of your income is going to come from 20 percent of your customers. Once you have a customer that you know is going to buy from you, there's a good chance that they'll be repeat buyers. If you aren't upselling or making offers to them for additional products, you're missing out on a lot of additional revenue and the opportunity to build a long-term relationship.

RICK:

❝ I first learned this lesson at a very young age. When I was just out of college, I worked as a lifeguard in Daytona Beach. I was on commission only, selling suntan lotion to people lying by the pool. If I didn't sell any lotion, I didn't get paid that day. Initially I had some small success selling people one bottle of basic tanning lotion for only $8. I quickly realized that the way to make more money was to upsell people on a complete "tanning system" of lotions and oils—a pre-tanning lotion, a tan accelerant, advanced tanning oil, post-tan moisturizer, and sunburn pain reliever, just in case. The total cost of that package was $89, and people were more much more inclined to purchase a complete package versus paying $8 for only one bottle. That was a valuable lesson I learned very early in my career and was able to use in all my other marketing campaigns since. You are always trying to increase the average order value for each customer, because that allows you to spend more on your marketing, which then increases product awareness and sales.

How do you think companies selling products on TV for $19.95 make money? Clearly very few of them would exist if that were all the revenue they generated. But once the customer goes online or calls in to purchase, they're offered a series of upsells or even monthly subscriptions. The average order value ends up being $75 or $80 per customer. With every product that we've mentioned in this book, we've always made an effort to build in beneficial upsells for additional products.

Another common example of structured upselling common in the marketplace today is in the info-product marketing you see in many ads on Facebook. Let me take you through an example:

My brother Steve wrote a book called *Clarity*. You might see an ad on Facebook for a free copy of *Clarity* that requires only that you pay a shipping/handling fee of $7.95. If you click on this offer, it takes you to a webpage or sales funnel where you might be offered a ninety-day planner for $39 (upsell number one). From that point, you might be offered a seminar course, for $495 (upsell number two). From there, you might be offered a webinar for $1,995 (upsell number three). At that point you might be offered a live, in-person "Destination Planning One-Day Session" for $24,495 (upsell number four), and then, if you qualify, you might be asked to join his MasterMind group for $35,000 year. With a series of smart upsells like that, you can see how what started out as a free book can escalate into a lucrative ongoing business. Of course, more value is being delivered at every next level of sales.

Your Upsell has to be Authentic.

Successful upselling requires you offer the consumer a product, service, or add-on to the product they just bought that makes sense for them, is priced right, and that appeals to their judgment and their emotion at the time of purchasing. That's critical to your success in terms of driving increased revenue. You've got to choose wisely and test, because not every add-on upsell is going to work. In the info-mercial world, some people try to cram every type of product into an upsell. If you buy one of those $19.99 pancake flippers, they try to do six upsells and the last one is something like joining a travel club that has nothing to do with pancake flippers.

This is very short-term thinking, and does not help in any way to build a brand. The more tied to the initial product that the follow-on products are, the better chance of success you're going to have. Amazon uses what's called glancing technology: as you're putting that product in your shopping cart on Amazon, you will see on the bottom toolbar, "Customers Also Viewed…" with a selection of five or six items on a scrolling carousel. This not only serves to validate your purchase, it lets you know that you're in good standing. People who are smart like you also considered these items. This plays on what is known as "social proof," or "the herd mentality." People feel more comfortable purchasing when they see someone else has purchased something. A lot of people don't want to be the pioneer, or the first one. Amazon ties your choice into, "Other people have purchased these things." That means it must be good. You feel safe doing it, and you know you're going to get some value. If Amazon does this with every purchase, why shouldn't you be offering upsells as well?

Timeless Marketing Tip 2: Learn from Other People's Experience

This is a statement that holds true in so many areas of business and life, but as it pertains to marketing it's pretty simple: see what other people are doing successfully and then do the same thing, only better! Let me give you some examples.

I was always interested in health and nutrition. I used to read a lot of magazines, books, and newsletters from a company called Rodale Press (they publish *Prevention* magazine). They created the most compelling direct mail pieces to sell their products, and the copywriting was both compelling and informative. So, when we were starting the Juiceman, I did some research and was able to track down the copywriter who wrote most of their health copy pieces. I reached out to him and had him create an eight-and-a-half by eleven-inch direct mail piece touting the benefits of juicing and why everyone should own a Juiceman juicer. We used that original mail piece to help generate millions in sales. We did not reinvent the wheel, but looked at something that was working in the marketplace and then adapted it to our product.

Early in my career I helped market real estate seminars. The leading companies at the time were using newspaper ads to promote their seminars, but one company was getting much larger crowds then the rest. It turned out that they were using a direct response infomercial to drive people to their seminars. When we were starting our business, we skipped the newspaper ads and went right to TV. We were able to build one of the nation's largest seminar businesses in just a few short years. Imitation is the sincerest form of flattery, and in marketing it can help you generate many more sales. Look what's working in the market place and then see how you can adapt it for your own products or business.

Timeless Marketing Tip 3: Zig When Others Are Zagging

We've talked in other chapters about a favorite book I often recommend when I'm speaking on stage or being interviewed, called the *Blue Ocean Strategy*. It's about positioning and how to find the "Blue Ocean" for your product—the place where nobody else is. This gives you open space in which to grow your brand and business with the least amount of competition. The authors W. Chan Kim and Renée Mauborgne have a new book out called the *Blue Ocean Shift*. I've simplified their message quite a bit, but all you need to know is that when you're launching a new product, look at what everyone else is doing, then do something different: zig when they zag. Look for a space in the marketplace where there's an opportunity to take over a niche or a field or a market where nobody else has staked a claim. Barb accomplished this with the George Foreman Grill when she decided to make its ability to "knock out fat" when cooking a benefit, because no other grilling appliance was talking about or delivering that health aspect of cooking. Sonicare offered to "clean beyond the bristles"; OxiClean promised "the power of bleach, but safe."

Timeless Marketing Tip 4: Features Tell, Benefits Sell

When we introduced the Juiceman juice extractor into the market, we were up against competition from some top German appliance companies, Braun and Krups, both of which are known for their quality engineering. Features like a powerful motor, stainless steel blades, and dishwasher safe plastic were what they chose to highlight in their advertising—all important attributes, but boring. But when we went to market we talked about the myriad benefits realized from the juice made by the machine: If you drink fresh juice you'll have more energy. You'll live longer. You can lower your blood pressure and cholesterol, and have better looking skin, hair and nails. Now, compare our selling message to Braun's and Krups'; which would you rather buy? Selling the benefits of the juice from the machine enabled us to dominate the marketplace over those other brands, even though we were just a small startup. As I told an interviewer for *Success Magazine*, "We don't sell people a juicer. We sell them a better lifestyle. We made our number one goal educating people. If we do a good job of education, the sales just follow." Think about that in terms of your product: "We don't just sell people a (your product). We sell them a better lifestyle."

Timeless Marketing Tip 5: Establish Credibility

Back in the '90s when we were doing the initial Sonicare infomercial, we were discussing who should host it, and Vanna White's name came up. She is the long-time co-host of the game show *Wheel of Fortune*. Vanna White is attractive—she has nice teeth; people like to see her smile. But we wound up going with an actor named Richard Dysart. Now, unlike Ms. White, Mr. Dysart didn't have perfect teeth. But he had an "everyman" appeal and credibility with the viewing public based on the role he played on the television series *LA Law*. On this very popular show, his character, Leyland McKenzie, is the head of the law firm. His character is honest, trustworthy, and credible. People believed what Richard Dysart said because he projected the same integrity and honesty his character had on the show. He was the perfect spokesperson for the product because we were looking for someone who was more than just another pretty smile; we were looking for a messenger with credibility, because the message we were delivering was serious one about gum disease and how this new product, Sonicare, used a new sonic technology to actually help reverse gum disease. The choice of host worked as Sonicare's revenue grew to over $200 million in just a few short years!

Timeless Marketing Tip 6: Leverage Key Opinion Leaders and Influencers

When experts speak, consumers listen—and when they praise your product, they lend important credibility (see tip number five). Sonicare's founders knew that having the stamp of approval from respected medical authorities would give their revolutionary (and expensive) toothbrush luster in the eyes of consumers, so when they first launched their toothbrush they sent out samples to all the top periodontists and dentists in the country, especially to academics at well-known dental schools. These key opinion leaders endorsed Sonicare as effective, and we wound up interviewing several of these experts (or as they're known today, influencers) for our brand response commercials.

GoPro founder, Nick Woodman, got his marketing started by sending GoPro cameras to top surfers, mountain bikers, motorcycle racers and other extreme athletes, people who could influence the market he was looking to reach and got them all using the product. The videos they made with the cameras and posted on YouTube became the main part of the GoPro marketing campaign and gave the product instant credibility with its target consumers—amateur extreme athletes who wanted to show off their exploits, just like their action sports heroes.

Experts and influencers are out there to be tapped in every product space; new beauty products, for instance, can gain altitude at launch if they get positive reviews from the people who attend BeautyCon, where makeup mavens meet to talk new products and come away from the event to blog and post YouTube videos on what they saw there.

Occasionally someone famous or influential will discover your product on their own, and you can reach out to that person to ask for an endorsement or get an implied endorsement because they like your product and mention it to their followers. One thing that helped propel the growth of both Sonicare and Clarisonic was that both of these products were picked as one of Oprah's favorite products.

I'm on the board of advisors for a company called Natural Stacks. When they initially launched their patented flagship product called CILTEP, they were endorsed by both author Tim Ferris (*The 4 Hour Work Week*) and Dave Asprey (*Bullet Proof Coffee*). Both of these top influencers have millions of followers who were influenced to try the products and helped get the business off to a successful start. The founders also noticed that Dr. Drew—a doctor who's frequently seen on TV shows as a medical expert and who has about three million Twitter followers—was a customer who had ordered and reordered the product because he liked it. He is another person whose endorsement can have a positive influence on sales.

Timeless Marketing Tip 7: Know Your Customer

Sometimes what might seem like a natural idea around marketing turns out to be less than effective because it doesn't reach the consumer you're aiming at. That happened to us when we were promoting the George Foreman Grill. In our initial TV commercial we included footage of George winning the Heavyweight Championship by knocking out Michael Moorer. He became the oldest person to ever hold the heavyweight title. I thought it would be cool to show footage of that victory, so I called up HBO and we paid $15,000 for ten seconds of footage. But it turned out that women were initial purchasers of the grill and they, in general, didn't like boxing. Since this footage was at the beginning of the spot, they quickly tuned out and there was very little sales activity. When we took the boxing footage out of the commercial and concentrated on the health benefits of cooking with less grease and fat, it sold much more quickly. This was a pricey lesson—it cost over $15,000 to make the changes, but it didn't appeal to our customer base, so out it went.

It's worth mentioning that the guys who ran the company initially loved the boxing footage and wanted it in the commercial—and that also cost them money in lost sales until they could be talked into taking it out of the commercial.

Timeless Marketing Tip 8: Use Authentic Testimonials

When an ordinary consumer tries your product and loves it enough to send you a testimonial, it establishes valuable third-party credibility you can use. This is taking word of mouth advertising to the next level. Ad agencies often hire actors to perform scripts that sound like testimonials, but they lack authenticity and can misfire with consumers, or simply leave them indifferent. You get authenticity when you go out and interview actual customers to find out what they really think. If it's a glowing review, find a way to feature that in your product marketing promotions. Great product or company testimonials should be used throughout the company website and in your PR and social media channels.

When weight loss and exercise guru Richard Simmons was promoting his diet products, we did a show for him where we interviewed some of the folks who'd lost weight using his program and products. It was a very moving, emotional show as these people shared their personal journeys to health; sometimes they would start crying on camera. That made for a compelling emotional experience that really connected with our viewers and helped move a lot of product.

If you have seen the new Chevy ads on TV, you'll notice they make a point of calling out that the people we are seeing in their ads are "real people, not actors" because viewers are looking for authenticity. It makes you wonder about all the ads they produced over the years before. Were those people somehow unreal?

Timeless Marketing Tip 9: Powerful "Before and After" Demos

If you can show people the improvement customers have experienced from using your product via before and after photos or videos, it makes a compelling argument for buying what you're selling. When we were promoting Sonicare, we used before and after shots of people who'd used the toothbrush for six weeks and had visibly whiter teeth. Weight loss and fitness programs have relied on before and after shots of customers forever, because that visual proof of effectiveness is more persuasive than any pitch could be. The answer was beauty products showing legitimate users with real improvements and looking more beautiful. Cleaning products use before and demos of stains or dirty surfaces then show them looking much cleaner after using the product. Oxiclean's most famous TV cleaning demonstration showed Billy Mays (my agency made Billy's very first infomercial for OxiClean) pouring iodine in a big tub of water with white sheets and towels, turning the water a vivid reddish brown. He would then pour in the OxiClean and the water would instantly turn clear. That one "magic" before and after demo helped sell millions and millions of dollars worth of the OxiClean product. It was similar to the demo made famous by a German cleaning product called DD7. The more I study marketing history, the more I realize that there really are no new ideas, just new products and different ways of presenting them.

Whenever a product can utilize an effective before and after demo, it's a highly effective tool for selling more product. **"**

BARB:

" For several years I worked on the development of a groundbreaking beauty product, DermaFlash, a unique and effective facial hair remover. The videos of women using the product are remarkable, because you can literally see the peach fuzz falling off their faces like tumbleweeds. It's a super successful product, led by a phenomenal visionary in the beauty world, Dara Levy. DermaFlash under Dara's vision and direction created a highly impactful social tool/fan base called the Flash Mob. Her user generated content is dynamic, engaging, and most of all believable, creating trust in and satisfaction with the results of using DermaFlash.

Dara is an exceptional example of a founder with vision, determination, and belief in her invention. Her success in creating a new category based upon a new solution with consumer acceptance is a beauty benchmark!

Timeless Marketing Tip 10: Make the Customer the Hero

If you have doubts that your customer wants to be seen as the hero or the star, consider the "selfie." The fact is, people love to see themselves in photos and videos, and they love to see likes and thumbs up review on their postings. The more customer-centric your advertising is the better, and there's no stronger case study for the truth of that than the previously-mentioned campaign for GoPro. GoPro's fans are encouraged to send the company their homemade sports videos, which can then be featured on their website, Youtube channel, and TV commercials. The customer is the star *and* the hero in each of these videos. BeachBody and their USG is phenomenal. Their fans and customers willingly take pictures of themselves with their love handles and belly bulges for their before, and of course, for their the testimonial laden after. Endorsements like these are priceless!

Your customer will relate to seeing someone who looks like them (rather than an actor) enjoying the benefits of your product. It doesn't matter if the product is beauty, fitness, a new dress, killer cool kicks, or a new recipe. The culture and world of user-generated content is here and it's not going away! The kicker—you don't have to have the tag: Actor portrayal on your ad.

The more that you can make the customer the center of the benefits that your product provides, the more powerful your pitch will be. 〞

If you can put these Ten Timeless Marketing tools to work for your product, your marketing has a much greater chance of persuading shoppers to become customers—*your* customers.

Authentic Testimonials

Using confirmed, authentic testimonials is one of the best ways to build and grow your brand. What better way to tell potential new customers or clients about your product or service than by using the testimonials of people who are already using your product? This works in print ads, sales letters, infomercials—you name it. In fact, Amazon uses the concept with their reviews for books and other products. I have many clients currently using video testimonials on Facebook that work better than any other ad they run.

From the very first moment you start selling yourself or your product, you should be collecting testimonials. For example, you could send out a "Tell us how we did" postcard to new customers with a grading scale and a final question along the lines of "Finally, what would you say to someone else considering using [your name / product name]?"

Every chance you get, gather feedback. Eventually, you'll have an entire library of testimonials. This is incredibly valuable. You'll find that you will have one that fits any type of advertising you do to any type of demographic.

Summary

Marketing generates sales, and sales are what build your brand. Try to implement as many of our timeless marketing tips as you can into your current marketing and watch your sales soar and your brand grow.

CHAPTER TEN

- -

The Power of Y

"People don't buy what you do; they buy why you do it. And what you do simply proves what you believe."
—Simon Sinek, *Start with Why: How Great Leaders Inspire Everyone to Take Action*

Simon Sinek, the author of *Start with Why*, talks about the power of "why" as the underlying reason for doing something in business, but we are going to have a little fun and look at ten important words that end in the letter Y and "why" they are important to your branding efforts. Whether you call it jargon, argot, or business terminology, the field of branding is rich with buzzwords. Some of them get thrown around pretty indiscriminately, which muddies their meaning. In this chapter we're going to clear the waters around some of the most important words and what they mean to you in your branding efforts. You can think of this as your "cheat sheet" to help jumpstart building your brand.

1. Authenticity

This is a flavor that never goes out of fashion, but that's never stopped branders from veering from it, always to their cost. Fake testimonials, may tempt you, and there are certainly unscrupulous people out there willing to write them for a price. But ultimately, when the truth comes out, any hope of conveying authenticity you might have had is gone for good.

How do you do authenticity right? Get your products into the hands of real people and get their honest feedback. We been using authentic testimonials for over twenty-five years and we frankly believe it is easier from a marketing perspective to let these real people do the selling than it is trying to think up clever statements or lines for actors to read from scripts. We've always found that you just can't write lines that ring as true or are as to the point as what your fans will say about your products.

The other place where authenticity is important is in your company's or your product's story. A great example of an authentic brand story to emulate is Nike. Think about where Nike got its start—from the track coach, Bill Bowerman, and his student athlete Phil Knight at the University of Oregon track team. Do you remember the original waffle trainers whose soles were actually made in a waffle iron? That's a true and powerful brand story. What is a powerful story you can tell about your brand?

2. Quality

The key to quality is quality control, and quality control is critical to brand engagement. If you're making blouses and the sizing varies wildly, that's a problem. Your customer counts on quality, but when her size no longer fits, even though her weight hasn't changed, it creates a physical disconnect with the brand. Without dependable quality, your customers can't depend on a satisfactory experience, and they're going to look elsewhere. Delivering a quality product every time is essential to creating brand loyalty. Remember most long term branding starts *after* the sale. Delivering quality goes a long way to helping build your brand.

3. Consistency

When it comes to branding, what matters is the consistency of your messaging: tell your customer the same thing in the same language until your name is synonymous with your message. A great example is Dyson vacuums. Since Dyson launched in the United States, their brand message has remained consistent: "Doesn't Lose Suction." The Foreman Grill's tagline was "Knocks Out the Fat." GoPro was always the two words together with a capital "G" and "P." No one was ever allowed to use it as two words, "Go Pro." These might seem like minor points, but over thousands of impressions it helps build the brand. The consistency of the messaging lets you drive the USP home so it stays in people's minds.

4. Credibility

Credibility is an intangible, yet highly prized, attribute for any marketer; without consumer trust, you don't have a chance. No matter how great your product or service is, consumers may need that extra push to overcome their inherent distrust of marketers trying to sell, sell, sell. There is a work-around that helps build credibility fast, and that is third-party validation. By tapping into respected or trusted people in a particular category or topic, you benefit by association and the expert's credibility bleeds over to your brand. Who better exemplifies this than Dr. Oz? No matter what scandal Dr. Oz gets tangled in, his impact only increases and the brands he promotes gain prominence by association.

What makes people believe your advertising claims? Listening to third-party experts or others consumers that trust and talk about the product benefits, and reading news stories that tie into your PR and lend your claims credibility. Back when we were doing seminars for Juiceman, the American Cancer Society had a poster that said, "Eat your fruits and vegetables." We'd bring that poster around to our seminars, and tell the people, "Juicing is a great way to get more fruits and vegetables in your diet, and that's great for your health. But you don't have to believe us; believe the American Cancer Society." That lent us a lot of implied credibility when the concept of juicing was relatively new. With the Sonicare toothbrush, we could say, "Don't take our word for it: The top dentists and periodontists that are using Sonicare are recommending it to their patients." One road to establishing credibility requires leveraging third-party experts whose message complements yours but may stop short of a direct endorsement.

Celebrity endorsements can work, but the celebrity has to have some demonstrated expertise in the realm for them to work. Alternately, an unknown personality can create credibility. The founder of a cosmetics company, IT Cosmetics, did appearances on QVC where she demonstrated her product's effectiveness on herself. She had very pronounced facial redness and rosacea; on camera, she'd apply her product and the audience could see that redness completely disappear. The product is only a couple of years old, but her credibility with women is so strong that she sold her company for a small fortune to L'Oréal.

5. Honesty

How can you build consumer trust without honesty? Remember the classic case in which the FTC exposed Campbell's Soups for false advertising? Campbell's was using clear marbles in the steaming bowls of soup they photographed for ads, creating the effect that the bowl looked chock-full of noodles and chicken, when in fact, in real life, you'd see mostly broth. That's the kind of damage your brand may never be able to survive. Additionally, we'd much rather hear the host on a direct response ad saying, "I'd never even heard of this product before I worked on this program, but I tried it, and boy, do I like it," than leading the audience to believe he's been using it forever. The first looks like an honest response; the second looks like baloney.

6. Exclusivity

This word's been weakened by overuse in the past, much as "luxury" has become an overused term in the past ten years. What does it really mean? If I'm in retail and I advertise that a product is exclusive to me, it means the vendor isn't selling them to anybody else and you can't get them anywhere else. When you're marketing your products, retailers or your store outlets want to have exclusive items so that they don't have price bashing and can protect their margins, so it's a very strategic term in marketing, as well as a very strategic term within product development. For example, Kitchen Aid comes out with mixers in fifteen colors, and Macy's says it's "their exclusive or theirs first," this means that you, the consumer, can't get it at Bed Bath and Beyond. Scalable, supportable differentiation helps channel-manage within the hierarchy of your retail rollout.

7. Loyalty

Customer loyalty is the "Holy Grail" of branding, the golden ticket we're all searching for. How can you create it for your brand? By consistently delivering authentic, high-quality experiences your customer can depend on. You build customer loyalty by delivering on your brand's promise.

The goal of all brands is to build a loyal following. But loyalty has to work both ways. Nespresso, for instance, used to show its appreciation to its customers by gifting those who'd hit a certain purchase level with a free box of chocolates or some new espresso cups—a curated gift, especially for them at the end of the year. Loyalty is a big push within the travel sector, which offers loyalty programs for many airlines and credit cards. A store like Sephora rewards frequent customers with gifts of samples. Be loyal to those who are loyal to you, and the bond will grow.

8. Transparency

"Transparency" is a huge buzzword right now, especially in the food and health products arena. Naturalstacks, the supplement company we mentioned earlier, publishes both the ingredients and the amount of each ingredient in every supplement they make right on their website; that's complete transparency, and it resonates with their health-conscious consumers. They are the first supplement company that we know of to have done this. Transparency like that goes beyond authenticity, as it says, "We have nothing to hide; we make great products and we're proud of them."

9. Identity

Establishing your brand identity is critical. What is the identity going to look and feel like? How will it stand out from the visual clutter to your customer who's walking down an aisle at Target? And how is your identity going to live within the brand as the brand matures and ages, and as you expand your product range? Calvin Klein is a great example, because the logo identity for that product has lived across categories, from fashion to cosmetics to fragrance to shoes to jeans and to home fashion. It doesn't matter if you're buying a pair of Calvin Klein jeans at a Macy's or dinnerware at Bloomingdale's, that logo identity is very clear, and when you open up a magazine, the identity of Calvin Klein speaks for all the attributes of the brand, and it never wavers; it still feels contemporary.

10. Visibility

It's hard to build your brand without expanded visibility. This is called brand awareness. The simplest way to heighten visibility is through increased sales. The best way to increase sales while building your brand is through brand response or transactional marketing.

In transactional branding and marketing, you're creating visibility with your advertising because you're using a direct response model in which, for every ad dollar you spend, you're trying to create a positive return on that investment. When you advertise, whether it's online or traditional channels, you're not only building the brand, you're giving the people the opportunity to buy. You're generating revenue at the same time you're building the brand, creating a snowball effect. On Facebook, you can advertise your product for $20 a week. If people are responding to those ads, from a revenue-generating standpoint you just keep taking the money you're making off of the advertising, putting it back in, and building the visibility up.

How visible is your brand, and how are you driving visibility across geographic and psychographic dimensions? How's your organic, PPC, remarketing, retargeting? Are you using influencers to extend your visibility? Without plenty of visibility, it's tough to build a great brand.

Summary

Wherever you are in your branding journey, know your "Y"s as well as your why.

CHAPTER ELEVEN

- -

Your Brand at Retail

"Retail is a customer business. You're trying to take care of the customer—solve something for the customer. And there's no way to learn that in the classroom or in the corner office."

—Erik Nordstrom, president, Nordstrom Direct

The global retail marketplace is changing rapidly, and the retail marketplace in the United States is changing at lightning speed. Within the framework of the total retail environment, there are less than twenty retailers of volume consequence, ones that can have a serious impact on your sales, and that's just at this writing. In the past year, we've seen multiple mall-driven specialty stores with two hundred fifty or more locations close. As we write this, there are over one thousand and five hundred large retail stores empty and available for lease thanks to store closures and consolidations. Yet, expansion *is* happening on your laptop, on your tablet, and on your phone.

Your Customer is Online. Are You?

There are very successful retailers today who, if they're being honest, will tell you that over half of their volume is being done online. Retailers like Amazon are gobbling up market share by driving shopping convenience. When you look at how to expand your brand at retail, is all your content being created and driven with an eye on the new digital marketplace? That means your video, your content creation, your community-build, your reputation, your visual assets, all these things that we've talked about in the book, must support that type of shopping experience. Your website, your social platforms, everything you create has to support digital. Yes, there are plenty of brick-and-mortar stores open, and you will still find consumers that like to go to a mall because it's entertainment for them, or because they like to browse in person. However, chances are they will browse and conduct what's called in the business "show-rooming." This translates to: go to the mall, look at product in the store, and then go home and buy it through which ever retailer has the best offer, lower price, loyalty points, and, of course, free shipping. It's so much more convenient to have UPS deliver it to your front door than for you physically carry it out to your car. Of course, we'll see how drop off lockers and drones factor into the emerging delivery landscape.

What Does This Mean to You as You Strive to Establish Your Brand with Consumers?

You're still going to pour time and attention into packaging and identity, but the next most important thing to consider are logistics. No, the "L" word isn't as sexy as building community and creating all those visual assets, but if you don't cover the logistics base, you may lose the game.

When you're creating your packaging, are you considering whether or not it will pass the drop ship test? Is it compliant with ISTA? Again, this isn't very sexy, but it's critical. And how does your product ship? If it doesn't ship well, and your customers receive it broken, or if the packaging is bashed in when they receive it, they'll blame *you*, not UPS. A crushed package creates an immediate emotional response from the consumer of, "Whoa. Is everything alright?"

Please do yourself a favor and study how supply chain and block chain impact your vertical. If you never, ever sell to a major retailer or even Amazon, this won't pertain to you. However, if you're dreaming big and want to grow, this is essential stuff.

If your product is also sold in stores, do your homework first. Is the product exciting and innovative enough to earn it placement on an end cap? Can you justify a dynamic, engaging point-of-purchase display, and are you creating a user experience that delivers on all those "Y"s—on the identity, on the exclusivity, on the authenticity? Does everything about it say, "Wow, I really need to have this? If it isn't in my house, I'm not cutting it with my friends"? People love having bragging rights about the products they buy.

Use Facebook's Powerful Sales Tools.

Facebook is not just about showing your kid at the soccer match and what you ate for dinner; it's about sharing what you've bought, where you've been, what you've spent. If you go onto Facebook today, you will see that many brands have a call-to-action button: "Shop Now." The consumers are on their Facebook page looking for ideas and thinking, "Look at this cool picture." Why not ask them to buy it right then and there? If you're not doing it, you're losing sales. An impulse purchase is still a purchase, and it's gotten a lot easier to act on impulse. We've talked to people who say, "We don't want consumers to make an impulse purchase of our product. We want them to be informed," but you know what? There are a lot of people that are waiving their Visa, MasterCard or AMEX in the air and saying, "Take me. I'm yours. Hook me up."

Harness the Power of Amazon.

No matter how you feel about Amazon, it's the ruling force in retail right now. How you interact on Amazon, whether through Seller Central or Vendor Central, is a strategic question. You can create a store front on Seller Central in most categories, and you can set up an account relatively quickly. While it's not a cure-all for sales woes, you will see sales when you list your product on Amazon. You'll still have to buy some of the basic skill sets that you would in any digital marketplace, meaning meta-tagging, keywords, and PPC. On the Amazon platform you'll do that through Amazon Marketing Services. It's a very robust sales platform, especially since they have such a significant number of Prime subscribers—Amazon's building loyalty to their followers.

Believe it or not, today there are still companies that won't sell on Amazon, and there are just as many that only sell their products on Amazon. We believe the best way to sell a product is to offer it anywhere the customer wants to buy it. In short, we are completely sales channel agnostic. If you start by developing a great product, you should make that product available to customers wherever they choose to buy it, whether that's online, in a store, or channels like the Home Shopping Network.

With its incredibly large selection, fast, free shipping, and an ever-growing suite of Prime digital services, now more than ever, shoppers are buying their products from Amazon. Amazon has created tremendous customer loyalty with its fast-growing customer base and many customers now start and finish their shopping on Amazon.com. In 2017, Prime membership topped ninety million customers, and in 2017, 60 percent of all product searches originated on Amazon rather than Google. By the beginning of 2018, Amazon will own half of all the online market share in the United States, and it's quickly expanding in the EU, Japan, India, South America, and other countries. Amazon truly has become "the internet of products."

Strictly Brick-and-Mortar Companies Face More Revenue Impact than You Think.

Sometimes people tell us, "I don't want to be on digital or on Amazon. I want to be in the stores." It's as though they think they can roll progress back to circa 1985, and they're not considering all the ramifications.

You want to be in the store? Okay. You're in the store. You spend a lot of money, you ship your goods in, you're on the floor. You've got your spot on the planogram, and you really feel like you're launched. Is it time to break out the champagne?

Not yet. What you may not have considered is that the retailer is going to hold your accounts payables for sixty days to make sure your goods are selling, because they don't want to get stuck owning your goods. That means you're not getting paid for sixty days; it's what is called "consignment on the sly." You have thirty days for your sales velocity to meet the store's standard, and if after that thirty days your goods are not selling at the store's standard minimum velocity, you're going to get a call on day thirty-two or so, saying, "Either come and pick it up, or we're marking it down, and you have to make us whole," meaning, "You have to pay us back." You *still* haven't been paid, by the way, but now you have to pay them back on margin. If they owed you $100,000, maybe now they'll tell you, "We only owe you $70,000." And if your goods *still* don't start selling, they do another markdown. Now they're going to say, "We only owe you fifty grand." *They still haven't paid you.* Brick-and-mortar retailing is a tough road to market these days. In the end, you're not seeing receivables for over ninety days, but you already bought the goods and probably paid the factory for them at least sixty days prior. Do you have the stomach for what becomes nearly five months of financing?

Is selling digitally starting to sound more attractive now?

Our advice? Go digital first, and then curate where you are at retail, because if you're a startup, can you really afford to go into brick-and-mortar? Yes, you may get a darn big order, but you have a darn big problem if it doesn't sell quickly enough.

Like it or not, the digital marketplace is here to stay. And for you, it's the smart place to start building your brand at retail and on your terms.

Like it or not, the digital marketplace is here to stay. And for you, it's the smart place to start building your brand at retail and on your terms.

Here's a solid starting point and perspective as to what constitutes this digital landscape:

- Owned and Operated (O+O): O+O is a broadcast term: These are portals where you own the URL or registered the page name and you and your team are entirely responsible for content creation and design. You're in the driver's seat and you outright own that car. What's the grade of gas you're putting in the tank?

- Your website, its scalability and robustness on desktop, laptop, mobile iOS, and Android views

- Site security and shopping cart functionality is critical. Can you upsell, cross sell, and stay linked with abandoned carts? Of course, you retarget.

- Database building via the site, and all social platforms

- Do you have an app? Does it integrate with your product and/or is it experiential? Is it shopable?

- Today it's Facebook, Instagram, Twitter, Pinterest, and Snapchat. Tomorrow? No matter the platform, is it shopable? Consumers will find the quickest, fastest route to quench their thirst for your goods. Ensure that the checkout stand is within one click!

- How do you rank on marketplaces? Are you on eBay? Seller Central and RevCascade among others?

- Are you working on IoT and AI functionality for your product? Does it warrant this, or is AI a non-factor? Why is this important? "Alexa, order me a dozen…"

With digital shopping events cropping up continually, and in bigger, more financially profound ways, if you're not digital, you are not on the bus. With all of this digital power at your fingertips, why even bother with traditional retailers and their ecom sites? For every one or two items you sell directly to the consumer, you will keep more cash for your margin and P+L. So with all of these plus column attributes, who needs the retailer anyway?

You do.

Yes, it's true—for every unit *you* sell directly, you keep more profit contribution dollars. Here's the caveat: How big is your SEO budget? How many site visits do you get per day? How's your bounce rate? Do you have an affinity and loyalty program? What's your outbound landscape like?

Summary

Like it or not, the digital marketplace is here to stay. And for you, it's the smart place to start building your brand at retail and on your terms. Keep your horizons open and realistic. Today it might not be conceivable for you to sell goods on Alibaba, but will you be ready when they arrive on your digital doorstep?

- Build a digital platform that is strategic and covers shopping across differing marketplaces. Make sure it's scalable. You don't want to crash because Ellen or Oprah tout your product.

- Curate your retail expansion. Make sure your company can live within the legal constraints of a vendor agreement.

- Make sure that your 3PL or warehouse can effectively run EDI and pick and ship so that you are in best practices from the first day you decide to move this operation out of your garage.

- Protect yourself, your company, and your brand reputation by (1) having proper liability insurance and (2) having friendly, knowledgeable people running consumer service. Great consumer service is a priceless part of your branding toolbox. So at the very least, install a ZenDesk function or live chat on your site.

CONCLUSION

RICK

❝ When you write a book you never quite know where it will lead, what doors it will open, what experiences it will bring, or what new people that you will meet. In 2011 when I finished my first book, *Buy Now: Creative Marketing that Gets Customers to Respond to You and Your Product,* it was distributed at Hudson Book Stores located in most of the major airports around the country. I was in my office in Seattle shortly after the initial release and the receptionist said that I had a call from somebody who just bought my book.

The gentleman told me he was on his way home to Cairo and had a layover in Miami when he bought my book and loved some of the marketing ideas that he read. He told me that his father was one of the largest real estate developers in Egypt, and he wanted to try using some direct response television commercials to sell condo units in two large developments his family owned in Egypt. He wanted to fly me over to Egypt to see the resorts and get a proposal from us to help them market the properties. Since he was in a hurry to catch his next flight, I took down his contact information and told him I would follow up.

I could write another book about all the events that happened to us over the next two months while taping these commercials, but let's just say it was one of the more interesting projects we ever worked on. Every script line was originally written in English, then translated into Arabic, then changed to match the actors' personalities on set. By the time the work was completed, I wasn't totally sure what was being said, but we finished the commercials and they aired all over the Arab-speaking countries and helped sell many condominium units.

Even on this project in a foreign country using a foreign language and selling a product worth several hundred thousand dollars, I followed our Five Keys to Building a Great Brand. What was the USP for this product? The resort was built around a golf course, in the middle of a desert. While there, I never saw anyone actually playing golf; with daytime temperatures around 110-115 degrees Fahrenheit, I could see why. I asked, "Why even build a golf course in the first place?" and was told it was because people were drawn to green grass around their property and would pay extra for the condo units. This was different than other properties being sold and this became our USP. We added great testimonials of current owners, put together a special package that created more value, and we had a winning campaign! 🙸

BARB

🙸 So just when did the idea of advertising and marketing come to life? In my opinion, the activation of grabbing attention began with cave paintings dating back forty thousand years ago. Symbols, (or what we savvy marketers refer to as "icons") of animals, weather, and geographical locations drawn by humans prevailed at that time. Basic human needs of shelter, food supply, and climate were shared with others. Our ancient ancestors were passing down knowledge and information.

Seemingly primitive, yet today we are communicating using emojis and that's about as symbolic as one can get! Okay, without a doubt, it's a zillion times faster using a smart phone than carving a rock. So when communication platforms and methods change lightning fast, will you be flexible enough in both your outlook and desire to reach customers so that your business moves with the needle, not against it?

To summarize, neither marketing communications nor advertising are "new." Thousands of years ago, early humans were letting their "crowd" know where the best hunting and gathering spots were, and how to locate them. Whether it's location, crowd communication, friend messaging, influencers, smoke signals, engravings, etchings, breadcrumbs—no matter the platform, it's always about getting the message across to others from your vantage point and convincing them that you've got the solution to what they are looking for and you're selling to them.

A few years ago, as I was walking through the awe-inspiring ruins of Ephesus in Turkey (a bucket list visit) and the guide explained that the carving in the pathway stones "pitched" the Romans on where to go for a good time. Those service providers wanted customers, and those customers were looking for a service. Carved into the massive slabs of rock we walked across was this very specific messaging regarding services to be offered for sale. Not so different an ad medium than giant floor stickers we see today in subways, stadiums, and shopping venues.

The takeaway we leave you with is to stay current, and when marketing platforms change, change with them. Failure is not an option? How about extinction is not an option! 🙶

RICK

🙶 I've now known Barb now for over twenty-five years, most recently spending a lot of fun time together working on this book at her beautiful house in the Provence area of France. We have worked on hundreds of D2C product launches both together and separately. How we market has changed dramatically over the years and one thing is certain: that will continue to change. What we have tried to do is focus on the fundamentals that have always worked for us and we believe will continue to work, regardless of the distribution channel or technology being used. We had a huge amount of success using video on TV to create awareness and sell products. Guess what the latest trend in marketing is? Using video for content on your website and YouTube, using video for your product listings on Amazon, and using video for your Facebook ads and Facebook Live. All these channels are more effective selling your product using video than just the printed word. Good video production, video product explanations, and video testimonials are not new, only the way in which people are receiving them is new.

So, what is the next billion-dollar brand? Maybe one of the companies or products Barb and I are working with right now or it could be your product or company. I think Norman Vincent Peale said it best: "Shoot for the moon and even if you miss, you'll land among the stars." 🙶

CONTACT US

RICK CESARI

Rick is a best-selling author, speaker, and consultant. He is available to help inventors, business owners, entrepreneurs, and Amazon sellers with their marketing and brand strategy.

www.rickcesari.com

rick@directbranding.com

Please follow Rick on social media:

linkedin.com/in/rickcesaridrtv/

facebook.com/rickcesaridrtv/

twitter.com/rickcesaridrtv

rickcesari.tv

BARB WESTFIELD

Barb is an in-demand consultant, working with inventors, early stage start-ups, as well as long-term established CPG companies.

barbwestfield@gmail.com

Please follow Barb on social media:

linkedin.com/in/barb-westfield-a2721a2